ORAL EXERCISES

IN

ENGLISH COMPOSITION

ORAL EXERCISES

IN

ENGLISH COMPOSITION

J. C. NESFIELD

GYAN

Published by

Gyan Publishing House
5, Ansari Road
Daryaganj, New Delhi-110002
Phone: 011-47034999, 9811692060
E-mail: books@gyanbooks.com

Distribution Network
gyanbooks.com
India, USA, Canada, UK, Australia

ISBN: 978-93-6208-623-5 (PB)
First Published, 1905

2nd Impression 2024

Printed at: Gyan Press, Delhi.

ORAL EXERCISES IN ENGLISH COMPOSITION
Author: J. C. NESFIELD

ORAL EXERCISES
IN ENGLISH COMPOSITION

ORAL EXERCISES

IN

ENGLISH COMPOSITION

J. C. NESFIELD, M.A.

AUTHOR OF 'ENGLISH GRAMMAR, PAST AND PRESENT,' 'MANUAL OF ENGLISH GRAMMAR AND COMPOSITION,' ETC.

MACMILLAN & CO., LIMITED

ST. MARTIN'S STREET, LONDON

NEW YORK : THE MACMILLAN COMPANY

1905

PREFACE

THAT English composition in its earliest stages can be better taught by oral than by written exercises is an impression that for some time past has been gaining ground in educational circles. It is hoped, therefore, that an elementary text-book, prepared as this has been on an oral basis, will not be deemed superfluous.

The examples for practice have been printed in a type larger than usual, so that the beginner may have no difficulty in reading them at sight. He will thus be able to give all his attention to doing whatever the heading to the exercise may require him to do, such as supplying omitted words, correcting errors of grammar or order, analysing sentences orally, recasting the form of sentences, substituting equivalent words, etc.

It is of course open to the teacher at any time to have some of these examples worked out by the student at the desk and shown up to him in writing; and this may be advisable at times for the sake of variety, or for purposes of revision after an exercise has been done orally, or for practice in spelling and penmanship.

The student who uses this book must not expect that because we have given two chapters on "Grammatical Rules bearing on Composition" and appended a large number of exercises to each of them, he can be spared the trouble of acquiring some knowledge of English grammar before he begins, especially a knowledge of Accidence, of the uses of the Parts of Speech, and a few leading grammatical principles. We have attempted in this little book to breathe some life into grammar by giving a great deal of practice in its forms and rules, but not to supply the place of a grammatical treatise.

J. C. NESFIELD.

CONTENTS

CHAPTER I.—SIMPLE GRAMMATICAL RULES BEARING ON COMPOSITION.

SECTION 1.—VERB AND SUBJECT.

1. Number and Person of Verb.—A verb must be in the same *number* and the same *person* as the noun or pronoun going before.

The noun or pronoun going before is called the **Subject.**

James comes. We come.

Here *James*, the Subject, is Singular, and therefore the verb *comes* is Singular also. Similarly *we*, the Subject, is Plural, and therefore the verb *come* is Plural also.

All *nouns* are followed by verbs in the third person. All *personal pronouns*, too, are followed by verbs in the third person, except "*I, we*" (1st person) and "*thou, you*" (2nd person).

Note 1.—A verb thus used in combination with a Subject is said to be "Finite," that is, "limited,"—limited to the number and person of its Subject. Such forms as *to come*, *coming*, *having come* are not Finite, because they cannot have a Subject.

Note 2.—The Singular form *thou* (2nd person) is not now in ordinary use. Instead of using *thou* with a Singular verb, we use *you* with a Plural verb in the same sense as if it were Singular; as "You, my *boy*, *are* playing too much."

Exercise on § 1.[1] (To be done orally and at sight.)

Is, am.

Put into **Plural** *number.*

1. He *is* here.
2. The gate *is* locked.
3. I *am* very tired.
4. Where *is* he going?
5. My book *is* lost.
6. I *am* very sorry for it.
7. The fish *is* swimming.
8. My tooth *is* aching.
9. My foot *is* sore.
10. The child *is* happy.

Are.

Put into **Singular** *number.*

1. Ten loaves *are* baked.
2. The rats *are* caught.
3. No boxes *are* here.
4. Where *are* the boxes?
5. Flies *are* very harmful.
6. We *are* very tired.
7. Why *are* they so careless?
8. The oxen *are* resting.
9. We *are* fond of play.
10. Birds *are* roosting.

Was.

Put into **Plural** *number.*

1. A sheep *was* grazing here.
2. That *was* a cool valley.
3. The child *was* asleep.
4. The egg *was* cracked.
5. When *was* I admitted?
6. How old *was* he?
7. A deer *was* in the wood.
8. His foot *was* sore.
9. There *was* no proof.
10. A wolf *was* seen there.

Were.

Put into **Singular** *number.*

1. Some men *were* hurt.
2. We *were* playing.
3. *Were* the thieves caught?
4. The horses' tails *were* cut.
5. These mice *were* caught.
6. The geese *were* not found.
7. We *were* absent.
8. The ponies *were* sent away.
9. The loaves *were* served up.
10. The ladies *were* seated.

---

[1] *To the Teacher.*—We advise the teacher to adopt the following method in this and all subsequent exercises. Let the student be made first to read the example *slowly* to the class as it stands, and then to read it out *slowly* to the class in its altered form. We lay great emphasis on the word *slowly* for three reasons—(1) By slow and distinct reading pronunciation can be taught as well as grammatical accuracy; (2) spelling is taught without effort by keeping each sentence well before the student's eyes; (3) mistakes might not always be detected, if the student is allowed to gabble. It is especially necessary that the *last* consonant of an inflected word should be distinctly sounded.

We have said that these and all subsequent exercises should be done "*at sight*," because the time of the class ought not to be wasted in preparing to work out such very easy examples. The students are supposed

Have, has.

Put into **Plural** *number.*

1. He *has* long been gone.
2. *Have* I seen you before?
3. *Has* the cat been found?
4. The thief *has* been caught.
5. I *have* done my best.
6. The glass *has* been broken.
7. The roof *has* been mended.
8. The loaf *has* been cut.
9. The wolf *has* been shot.
10. The mouse *has* run away.

Have.

Put into **Singular** *number.*

1. The geese *have* been found.
2. My teeth *have* been aching.
3. His sons *have* left him.
4. We *have* left school.
5. The oxen *have* come back.
6. We *have* arrived.
7. The deer *have* fled.
8. The birds *have* flown.
9. The sheep *have* been lost.
10. My feet *have* been in pain.

Do, does.

Put into **Plural** *number.*

1. I *do* not like him.
2. He *does* not like me.
3. *Does* the boy work hard?
4. The boy *does* not know me.
5. A goose *does* not fly.
6. *Does* my friend know me?
7. *Does* the fire burn well?
8. He *does* not learn much.
9. *Does* he keep a dog?
10. The man *does* not work.

Do.

Put into **Singular** *number.*

1. We *do* not go to-day.
2. *Do* they keep a horse?
3. They keep a horse; so *do* we.
4. We *do* not understand you.
5. They *do* not go to school.
6. *Do* they wish to see me?
7. Wolves *do* not come here.
8. Our cows *do* not thrive.
9. We *do* not see you often.
10. We *do* not want your help.

2. Two Singulars connected by "and."—When two Singular nouns are connected by *and*, the verb is Plural:—

Time and tide *wait* for no man.
James and I *were* both absent.

---

to have learned something about grammar before this book is commenced. Previous preparation is condemned, not merely for the sake of saving time, but because promptness and facility must be acquired for composition.

Exception :—

If the two nouns are intended to express *one* person or thing, so that the Subject taken as a whole is Singular in *sense*, the verb is Singular also :—

Truth and honesty *is* the best policy.
This carriage and pair *costs* four hundred pounds.
The poet and statesman *is* dead.

Note.—If for "The poet and statesman" we say "The poet and *the* statesman," the repetition of the article shows that the statesman and the poet are two different persons. Since *two* different persons are mentioned, the verb must, of course, be plural. The sentence will then be—

The statesman and *the* poet *are* dead.

Exercise on § 2. (To be done orally and at sight.)

Insert **is, am** *or* **are, has** *or* **have, was** *or* **were, do** *or* **does** :—

1. Bread and butter —— a good kind of food at tea-time.
2. A woman and a child —— standing by the door.
3. A time of peace and plenty —— coming to all of us.
4. The head and front of your failure —— been laziness.
5. The black and the white kitten —— dead.
6. You and he —— late for school to-day ; why —— that?
7. The black and white kitten —— asleep.
8. The carriage and pair —— bought at a high price.
9. Snow mixed with rain —— falling, when I started.
10. The long and sort of the matter —— that he was angry.
11. James and I —— had a long walk to-day in the fields.
12. The sum and substance of all he says —— no effect.
13. A bay and a grey horse —— just been bought.
14. The cat and the dog —— long been good friends.

15. The horse and its rider —— not seem to be tired.
16. A short and unbound book —— not cost much.
17. A bunch of roses —— not satisfy him.
18. Bread and cheese —— not suit his taste.
19. Potatoes —— not grow well in heavy soil.
20. The cow and her calf —— not belong to me.
21. My pen —— been lost; —— you seen it?
22. Youth and experience —— not exist together.
23. The best painter and poet of this century —— lately died.

3. Two Singulars connected by "or," "nor."—When two Singulars are connected by *either* . . . *or*, or by *neither* . . . *nor*, the verb is Singular:—

Either James or John *is* to be promoted.
Neither James nor John *is* to be promoted.

Precautions:—

(*a*) When one of the Subjects is Singular and the other Plural, put the Plural subject last and make the verb Plural:—

Neither he nor his partners *were* present.

(*b*) When the Subjects are not of the same person, the verb takes the person and number of the Subject that stands nearest to it:—

(1) Either James or I *am* to get the prize.
(2) Either you or James *is* to get the prize.

But it is always possible to repeat the verb:—

(1) Either James *is* to get the prize, or I *am*.
(2) Either you *are* to get the prize, or James *is*.

Exercises on § 3. (To be done orally and at sight.)

(*a*) *Insert* **is, am** *or* **are, was** *or* **were, has** *or* **have, do** *or* **does**:—

1. That cloud shows that snow or rain —— about to fall.
2. Neither the cock nor the hens —— in the yard.

3. By what time —— you or your father decided to go?
4. One or two apples —— been picked up ripe.
5. Neither the man nor his wife —— much work.
6. Neither moon nor stars —— visible in this dark night.
7. To what place —— the man or his son wish to go?
8. Neither the master nor his pupils —— idle.
9. Neither he nor you —— heard of this before.
10. No girl or boy —— allowed to play in school.

(*b*) *Reproduce the following sentences so as to give two verbs in place of one*:—

1. Neither the farmer nor you have any right to be here.
2. Either you or your brother is expected to come.
3. Neither he nor you are deserving of any praise.
4. Neither he nor I have much work to do.
5. Neither you nor he does the work required.
6. Either he or you are to blame; perhaps both of you.
7. Neither my father nor I have seen him before.
8. Either the boy or I am to be blamed for this.
9. Neither he nor you were asleep at such an hour.
10. Neither my partner nor I have ever seen you before.

4. Two Singulars connected by "as well as."— When two Singular subjects are connected by *as well as*, the verb is Singular:—

A box as well as a book *has* been lost.

Precaution:—

If the two subjects differ from each other in number or person or both, the verb takes the number and person of the Subject that stands *first*:—

(1) My partners as well as I *were* ruined.
(2) I as well as they *am* tired of this work.

These sentences might be rewritten as follows, the verb being mentioned twice, once for each Subject:—

(1) I *was* ruined and so *were* my partners.
(2) They *are* tired of this work, and so *am* I.

Exercises on § 4. (To be done orally and at sight.)

(*a*) *Insert* **is, am** *or* **are, was** *or* **were, has** *or* **have, do** *or* **does** :—

1. This horse as well as that —— for sale; which will you have?
2. The horse as well as the rider —— hurt by the fall.
3. James as well as I —— won a prize this term.
4. I myself as well as James —— won a prize this term.
5. Beauty as well as wealth —— fallen to her lot in life.
6. The cock as well as the hens —— calling for food.
7. The hens as well as the cock —— calling for food.
8. A garden as well as a stable —— attached to the house.
9. A garden as well as stables —— attached to the house.
10. Stables as well as a garden —— attached to the house.

(*b*) *Reproduce the following sentences so as to give two verbs in place of one* :—

1. The jury as well as the judge are convinced of his guilt.
2. A horse as well as cows is needed for this farm.
3. Her good looks as well as her voice are much admired.
4. John as well as his friends was present on that day.
5. The moon as well as the stars is shining brightly.
6. He as well as you deserves to be blamed for this.
7. The pupils as well as the master have worked hard.
8. My father as well as I is a stranger in this place.
9. Stables as well as a cow-shed are needed here.
10. The keeper as well as the cows was drenched with rain.

5. Two Singulars connected by "not only" . . . "but also."—When two Singulars are connected by *not only* . . . *but also* or *but*, the verb is Singular :—

Not only England, but all the world *feels* the loss.

Precaution :—

If the two Subjects differ from each other in number or person or both, the verb takes the number and person of the Subject that stands *last* :—

Not only he, but his servants *were* blamed for that.

Such a sentence might be rewritten as follows, the verb being mentioned twice, once for each Subject :—

He *was* blamed for that, and so *were* his servants.

Exercises on § 5. (To be done orally and at sight.)

(*a*) *Insert* **is** *or* **are, has** *or* **have, was** *or* **were, do** *or* **does** :—

1. Not only silver, but gold —— dug in this country.
2. Not only my sister, but I myself —— much surprised.
3. Not only my sister, but my brothers —— been invited.
4. Not only the Thames, but the Severn —— frozen over.
5. Not only cows, but a horse —— grazing in that field.
6. Not only a horse, but cows —— grazing in that field.
7. Not only elm-trees, but ivy —— growing well here.
8. Not only I, but my children —— been disappointed.
9. Not only hope, but confidence —— been restored.
10. Not only bread, but tea and buns —— provided.

(*b*) *Reproduce the following sentences so as to give two verbs in place of one :—*

1. Not only the stars, but the moon is shining bright.
2. Not only the mother, but the children are ill with fever.
3. Not only my neighbours, but I myself am displeased.
4. Not only the king, but his subjects are made to suffer.
5. Not only his horse, but his oxen have been stolen.
6. Not only the flowers, but even the grass is withered.

7. Not only his threats, but his promise was carried out.
8. Not only your friend, but you yourself were praised.
9. Not only the hounds, but the huntsman has lost his way.
10. Not only the earth, but the planets move round the sun.

6. Noun of Multitude.—A noun in the Singular number, if it is used in a Plural sense so as to imply several persons or things taken separately, is followed by a Plural verb:—

The *people* who saw this *were* astonished.
The *jury were* divided in their opinions.

Here *people*, though a noun in the Singular number, stands for "persons." The *jury* here means the men who sat on the jury. Both nouns therefore have a Plural sense.

Precaution:—

If the noun denotes the collection *taken as a whole* rather than the individual persons or things that make up the collection, the verb is Singular:—

The *jury consists* of twelve persons.
This *firm has* a wider connection than that.

Exercise on § 6. (To be done orally and at sight.)

Insert **is** *or* **are**, **was** *or* **were**, **has** *or* **have**, **do** *or* **does**:—

1. Your pack of hounds —— larger than mine.
2. The pack —— scattered about in various places.
3. That fleet —— not consist of more than ten ships.
4. The people —— much amused at that sight.
5. That gang of seven thieves —— been broken up.
6. The gang —— nearly all caught: only two escaped.
7. The choir —— not contain more than ten choristers.
8. The choir —— all here and —— taken their usual seats.

9. The audience —— too large for a hall of that size.
10. The audience —— much pleased with his singing.
11. The company —— so excited that they rose from their seats.
12. The A.B.C. Company —— formed a few years ago.
13. The cattle —— out grazing in the field.
14. The fourth class with few exceptions —— done well.
15. The class —— too large to be taught by one man.
16. The poultry —— much mischief among flowers.
17. The gentry of this place —— not like dirty roads.
18. The mass of mankind —— much influenced by their surroundings.
19. The crew —— not cousist of more than twenty sailors.
20. The crew —— standing in different parts of the ship.

7. Position of Subject.—The two main rules to be observed are:—

(*a*) In stating or denying anything, the Subject stands first.

(*b*) In asking a question, the Subject never stands first, but is placed after some Auxiliary verb.

	Stating a Fact.	*Asking a Question.*
Forms of Present	He comes.	Does he come?
	He is coming.	Is he coming?
	He has come.	Has he come?
	He has been coming.	Has he been coming?
Forms of Past	He came.	Did he come?
	He was coming.	Was he coming?
	He had come.	Had he come?
	He had been coming.	Had he been coming?
Forms of Future	He will come.	Will he come?
	He will be coming.	Will he be coming?
	He will have come.	Will he have come?
	He will have been coming.	Will he have been coming?

Observe that in those sentences, in which a question is asked, the Present and Past tenses (Indefinite) are formed with the help of the Auxiliary *do* and *did*; as "Does he come?" (Present), "Did he come?" (Past).

Exercises on § 7. (To be done orally and at sight.)

(*a*) *Convert the following sentences from Assertive to Interrogative*:—

1. A boy was set to watch a flock of sheep.
2. He was told to cry out "Wolf!" if he saw a wolf coming.
3. The men ran to help him, when they heard him shout "Wolf!"
4. The boy laughed at them and thought he was very witty.
5. One day a wolf really came, and then the boy began to shout.
6. The men thought it was only one of his old tricks.
7. He shouted, and cried, and begged them to come to his help.
8. But no one would go to him or give him any help.
9. The wolf caught two sheep and a lamb, and killed them.
10. Those who raise false alarms will get no help when help is needed.
11. Men would soon die if they did not get food.
12. Milk is the best food for the young of most animals.
13. A great deal of food is taken from plants.
14. Many years have passed since we saw you last.
15. He will have reached home before the rain sets in.
16. He comes home for the holidays in ten days' time.
17. He has found the house that he was looking for.
18. You were going to tell me about your son's health.
19. A horse and cart will be passing along here soon.
20. They have been gathering in the hay all day long.
21. He was much pleased with this year's harvest.
22. He had scarcely time to pack up his things before starting.

(*b*) *Convert the following sentences from Interrogative to Assertive* :—

1. Have you found that kind of plant which grows in sand ?
2. Did he see the event that he has described so well ?
3. Does he like the scent of the rose as much as the flower ?
4. Will they remain much longer in this lonely place ?
5. In hot countries do men chiefly wear cotton garments ?
6. Did the shepherd drive away the wolf from the flock ?
7. Did he shear as many as ten sheep yesterday ?
8. Will she wear the same dress that she wore before ?
9. Did he write those splendid lines that I have just heard ?
10. Does an elephant live for a hundred years ?
11. Is an elephant the largest of all land-animals ?
12. Does this seem to be a fit reward for all your work ?
13. Could he have done all this without assistance ?
14. Did not the shepherd say that the sheep had strayed ?
15. Should he not take his place among the rest ?
16. Must we really start at this early hour ?
17. Did he stand all day in the open air ?
18. Does the sun rise at six in this season of the year ?
19. Did she awake and get up when she was called ?
20. Did you see by chance some one passing this way ?

8. Precautions.—Before closing this section, we wish to put the student on his guard against a few errors that are commonly heard among certain classes, and to explain a few other points :—

(*a*) **You was.**—This is very bad English. *You* is Plural ; and therefore, even when it refers to a single person, the verb must be Plural :—

Whereabouts *was* you ? (Change *was* to *were.*)

(*b*) **With.**—When we say "A man with his dog," this means the same as "A man and his dog." But the former must be followed by a Singular verb; the latter by a Plural one.

(1) A man with his dog *have* come. (Change *have* to *has*.)

This is wrong, because there is only one subject "man"; and since *man* is Singular, the verb must be Singular.

(2) A man and his dog have come.

This is right, because here there are two Subjects connected by "and"; see § 2.

(*c*) In such sentences as the following, take care to make the verb agree with its true Subject, and not with the noun that happens to be nearest to it:—

(1) The bundles of hay *is* out in the rain. (Change to *are*.)

This is wrong, because *bundles* is the Subject, not *hay*.

(2) A wall hung with pictures *charm* the eye. (Change *charm* to *charms*.)

This is wrong, because *wall* is the Subject, not *pictures*.

(*d*) **News.**—This noun, although it is Plural, is followed by a Singular verb. This is against the rule given in § 1. But we cannot help it: we have to follow the custom of the best writers.

Good news *has* come this morning. (Right.)

(*e*) **Number, variety.**—These nouns, though Singular in form, can be followed by a Plural verb, when they are used in a Plural sense:—

A great variety of articles *were* sold. (What was sold? Not variety, but *articles* of various kinds *were* sold.)

A large number of them *were* present. (What was present? Not number, but *they* who made the number *were* present.)

But when these nouns are used in a Singular sense, the verb is Singular:—

The number of workmen *is* small.
Variety of scene *pleases* the eye.

(*f*) **None.**—This is a contraction of *no one;* and should therefore be followed by a Singular verb. But when several persons or things are spoken of, the verb following is usually Plural:—

None of them *have* come. (Right.)

Here the verb is Plural, because the mention of "them" implies plurality.

(*g*) **Each, every; either, neither.**—The noun following these adjectives is Singular; and therefore the verb following such a noun must be Singular also:—

Each (man) of them *was* present. (Right.)
Every bush and every tree *was* in bud. (Right.)
Neither (man) of these men *are* wanted. (Wrong.)
Every bush and every tree *were* in bud. (Wrong.)

(*h*) A Plural noun, when it represents a single quantity or mass, or when it is the title of a book, is followed by a Singular verb:—

The *Adventures* of Robinson Crusoe *is* an interesting book.
Seven hundred *pounds* a year *is* a good income.

Miscellaneous Exercises. (To be done orally and at sight.)

(*a*) *Correct or justify the following sentences:*—

1. You was rather late in coming to school to-day; wasn't you?

2. Good news have come to-day; the enemy's troops are beaten.

3. Neither reward nor punishment are to be expected from him.

4. Nothing but dismal swamps lie before our path.

5. A carrier with his horse and dog have just entered the yard.

6. Every man and every horse were urgently needed.

7. Are either of these horses yours? No; neither of them are.

8. Not a word of these lectures were read out from a book.

9. None of the men selected was found fit for that purpose.

10. A large number of cattle is grazing in that field.

11. The audience was not agreed on that point.

12. The carriage and the horse is both worth a good deal.

13. When pain or grief attack us, we knows true friends from false.

14. The poultry in our yard is picking up seed.

15. I likes good dry weather for cutting grass.

16. There's four or five persons coming over to-day.

17. A white and a grey rabbit has run across the field.

18. There's as many as fifty sheep grazing on this moor.

19. The poet and painter that lived here are dead.

20. Either James or you is sure to win the first prize.

21. My box as well as my book have been taken away.

22. The sum of twenty shillings a week were paid to him.

23. A garden full of flowers look very beautiful.

24. I myself as well as my partners were at fault.

25. They, and not he, has to pay the fine which is due.

26. Both are clear writers; neither of them make mistakes.

27. Every man of the boat's crew except two were taken ill.

28. Oil with good lamps are the means used for lighting the house.

29. A large number of men has come asking for work.

30. To write well, to speak well, or to act well are difficult.

31. Energy and hopefulness, like faith, removes mountains.

32. Each and all of them was shocked at what they heard.

33. Dogs as a general rule is more faithful than cats.

34. Nothing but rain and clouds were seen on that day.

35. His tears runs down his beard, like winter's drops.—*Tempest*, v. 1, 16.

36. Neither he nor his friend were clever enough to find that out.

37. The sum and substance of the matter were that he was wrong.

38. To make this field fertile much digging and draining is needed.

39. True courage with hopefulness were displayed in his character.

40. The danger of delays have been much insisted on.

41. Every tree and every bush were breaking out into leaf.

42. The number of men employed were very great.

43. Whereabouts was you, when my letter reached you?

44. The gentry living here sees no harm in this practice.

45. Neither he nor I has anything to do with this matter.

46. A black and white kitten have come into the house.

47. The horse and its rider seems to be rather tired.

48. The mother with two children are standing outside.

49. Every person both old and young were admitted.

50. There are a score of handsome shops in this town.

51. The quickness of the general's movements are wonderful.

52. The habit of looking for and noticing small matters of detail help to make a man trusted.

53. How old was you on your last birthday?

54. He comes; nor heat nor cold his course delay.—JOHNSON.

55. Two sheep were found lying on the grass, and neither were alive.

56. Untimely storms makes men expect a dearth.—*Richard III.*, ii. 3, 33.

57. Three parts of him is ours already.—*Julius Cæsar*, i. 3, 154.

58. She lifts the coffer-lids that close his eyes,
Where, lo! two lamps, burnt out, in darkness lies.
Venus and Adonis, 1128.

59. There is no more such masters.—*Cymbeline*, iv. 2, 371.

60. Has his daughters brought him to this pass?—*King Lear*, iii. 4, 65.

61. The heaviness and guilt within my bosom
Takes off my manhood.—*Cymb.* v. 2, 1-2.

62. Plenty and peace breeds cowards.—*Cymb.* iii. 6, 21.

63. My hand and ring is yours.—*Cymb.* ii. 4, 57.

64. The number of Jews in the Russian army are equal to half the whole of the British army.—*Pearson's Weekly*, p. 10, Nov. 18, 1899.

65. Neither Lord C. nor Mr. F. seem to have realised the fact.—*Fort. Review*, p. 672, April 1900.

66. A number of cattle was captured.—*Daily Express*, p. 5, May 29, 1900.

67. The news were at length announced.—*Heart of Midlothian*, ch. iii.

68. To every word of praise there is added two of blame.—*Rev. of Reviews*, p. 391, April 1900.

69. Plaintiff's horse and cab was overturned, the horse being severely injured, and the cab smashed.—*Morning Post*, p. 4, Feb. 28, 1900.

70. His reading of the signs are hesitating and narrow.—Quoted in *Rev. of Reviews*, p. 178, Aug. 1900.

71. He was alive in A.D. 96, but the time and manner of his death is unknown.—REBER, *Christ of Paul*, p. 324.

72. Neither of the sisters were very much displeased.—THACKERAY.

73. The strength and vitality of any nation lies to no small degree in "the sons of the soil."—*Daily Express*, p. 4, Feb. 19, 1901.

(*b*) *Insert* **is** *or* **are, was** *or* **were, has** *or* **have, do** *or* **does** *in the places left blank:*—

1. The number of new members —— risen from ten to fifteen.
2. Every man who saw that —— expected to give evidence.
3. Either wine or beer —— less refreshing than pure water.
4. A man and his wife —— about to take the house opposite.
5. A cat with two kittens —— making much noise in the night.
6. Bread and butter —— given out for breakfast and tea.
7. Each of my brothers —— made a good start in life.
8. Neither bird nor beast —— seen in his garden.
9. Every one —— his troubles at some time or other.
10. The house with all his goods and chattels —— burnt down.
11. The crowing of the cocks on the roosts —— very loud.
12. There —— still ten people asking for tickets: —— we any left?
13. The tea-dealer and tallow-chandler —— not at home.
14. The tea-dealer and the tallow-chandler —— expected shortly.
15. Some people —— not like being told, when they are wrong.
16. The taste of these apples and pears —— excellent: buy some.
17. A number of boys —— come to see the cricket match.
18. The number of boys present —— about fifty.
19. The apples on every tree —— now ripe enough to be picked.
20. Either the farmer or his men —— not understand their work.

21. Either you or he —— to be dismissed to-morrow.

22. A large quantity of fruit of various kinds —— been bought.

23. A red and white handkerchief —— found in my drawer.

24. A red and a white handkerchief —— found in my drawer.

25. That woman with a child in her arms —— in need of help.

26. Industry, not ability, —— the secret of success.

27. Either Charles or I —— to be blamed for this accident.

28. The band of musicians —— all here, ready to begin.

29. The black and white kitten —— a great favourite in the house.

30. The black and the white kitten —— been given away to a neighbour.

31. The farmer as well as the labourers —— hard at work.

32. Not only the farmer, but the labourers —— hard at work.

33. Neither my son nor I —— pleased with this climate.

34. Either of these books —— well worth buying and reading.

35. The teaching as well as the maintenance of the child —— been thrown on the mother: the father —— a bad man.

36. A box of shells with two shillings —— picked up off the pavement.

37. The number of spectators —— not less than four thousand.

38. Neither your horse nor mine —— been ridden for two days.

39. The attendance of pupils —— much increased.

40. Not only ten shillings, but a pound —— been stolen from me.

41. A bunch of grapes as well as two apples —— given him.

42. The committee —— divided in their opinions.

43. The committee —— decided to do this by a majority of four.

44. A vase filled with pinks and roses —— placed on the table.

45. Neither of the two boys —— likely to be promoted.

46. Each of them —— very careless, and neither —— his best.

47. There —— a number of good things to be got in that shop.

48. None of the ships —— rescued from that fearful storm.

49. The sum and substance of the matter —— that we must pay.

50. Curry and rice —— a favourite dish in India.

51. To write, to speak, or to act —— not seem difficult.

52. Two men applied for the post, and neither —— accepted.

53. The news just brought —— expected yesterday.

54. Every tree —— cut down; every branch —— lopped off.

55. You —— very angry with me for saying what I did.

56. Neither of the sisters —— much admired for her singing.

57. A thousand more horses —— been shipped to South Africa.

58. The sound of drums and fifes and trumpets —— heard.

59. Industry, not natural cleverness, —— been the cause of his success.

60. Either he or his friends —— to be invited.

61. Either his friends —— to be invited, or he ——.

62. Neither of the answers that he gave —— right.

63. None of the battles fought —— a decisive victory.

64. None of the prisoners —— released on that day.

65. Neither Charles nor his sister —— in good health.

66. The *Tales of a Grandfather* —— one of Scott's novels.

67. Thirty shillings a week —— good pay for a labourer.

68. The *Lives of the Poets* —— a book written by Dr. Johnson.

69. A large number of waggons —— captured.

70. The number of students in this class —— too large.

71. The cattle —— grazing in the field.

72. Poultry —— very mischievous in a garden.

73. The audience —— much pleased with her singing.

74. There —— about sixty students in this school.

75. Either of these novels —— well worth reading.

76. The great orator and statesman —— dead.

77. The black and the white kitten —— been killed by a dog.

78. A black and a white kitten —— found in the garden.

Section 2.—Affirmative and Negative Sentences.

9. Affirmative and Negative.—To express the negative forms of a Present tense, as *comes*, or of a Past tense, as *came*, we make use of the verb *do* or *did*; as—

	Affirmative.	*Negative.*
Present	1. I come.	1. I do not come.
	2. You come.	2. You do not come.
	3. He comes.	3. He does not come.
Past	1. I came.	1. I did not come.
	2. You came.	2. You did not come.
	3. He came.	3. He did not come.

Exercises on § 9. (To be done orally and at sight.)

(*a*) *Convert the following sentences from Affirmative to Negative* :—

1. He expects to see improvement the next time he calls.

2. I expect to see much improvement in a week's time.

3. I felt much surprised at what I saw.
4. You sang better yesterday than to-day.
5. We heard of your success from your father.
6. The sun came out bright in the early hours of the morning.
7. It rained hard at twelve o'clock.
8. The leaves look fresh and green, and the air smells sweet.
9. I thought that you would come by four in the afternoon.
10. The bees gathered much honey from those flowers.
11. This tree strikes its roots deep into the ground.
12. Some trees die before they are a hundred years old.
13. They told the boy to keep watch over the flock.
14. He strove to do his very best in his new class.
15. He gave as much as sixpence for that little book.
16. The fox fell into the trap that was laid for it.
17. The sun rose at six o'clock this morning.

(b) *Convert the following sentences from Negative to Affirmative :—*

1. He did not see the wolf secretly entering the field.
2. The sun does not rise at five o'clock.
3. The watchman did not run away from the thief.
4. We did not think John to be as clever as James.
5. He did not speak about the coldness of the class-room.
6. I do not think that a complaint should be made.
7. Bees do not gather much honey from these flowers.
8. He did not sing as well to-day as yesterday.
9. He did not feel ill during his absence from home.
10. The lightning did not strike the top of the house.
11. The noise in the street did not break my sleep.
12. This student did not strive to keep at the head of the class.
13. The child, walking along the bank, did not fall into the river.
14. I do not see how you will be able to do this.

15. He does not come here in time for his dinner.
16. They did not seek for the lamb that had been lost.
17. The dogs did not hunt the deer without success.
18. The master does not expect me to finish this all at once.
19. This book does not seem to be as interesting as that.
20. He did not hear, I think, all that I said to him.

10. Double Negative.—A sentence, which is intended, not to affirm, but to deny something, must contain only *one* word or phrase to express the denial. If two negatives are used, the second destroys the first, and makes the sentence affirmative. Thus "not unworthy of a prize" means "worthy of a prize."

I can*not* walk *no* further to-day. (Change *no* to *any*.)
That will not stop him; *nothing never* did. (Change *never* to *ever*.)

Exercise on § 10. (To be done orally and at sight.)

If you find a double Negative in any of the following sentences, remove it:—

1. I will not give this man none of my money, if I can help it.
2. Nobody hardly knew what was the matter with him.
3. You will not be allowed to come in here,—not by no means.
4. I will not do such a thing, neither now nor at any other time.
5. It is not going to rain to-day, I don't think.
6. With outstretched hoe I slew him at the door,
   And taught him never to come there no more.
   COWPER.
7. Never, neither at home nor abroad, did he waste his money.
8. You may deny that you were not the cause.—SHAKSPEARE.

9. I forbade you not to enter this room.
10. He said he would not come home no more.
11. No one scarcely knew what he was going to say.
12. No praise or blame never made him change his mind.
13. No Scotchman, nor Englishman neither, will act in that way.
14. No watchman has found the thief, and probably no one never will.
15. Here we have to wait, not so very long neither.
16. No change of clothes made him look no better.
17. I am not by no means as clever as he is.
18. She does not intend to do no sewing to-day.
19. He is left without no hope, as he has lost everything.
20. Neither pity nor friendship nor no such thing cheers him.
21. Be hopeful, nor take no thought for the morrow.
22. We did not nor do not believe what they say.
23. Haven't none of you heard nothing about that accident?
24. I have received no letter, neither from him nor from her.
25. No fruit hardly is ripe yet: summer isn't hardly come.
26. "Nay then," said the gardener, "I was not idle neither."

11. Precautions.—There are certain negative forms, in the use of which the student should be especially careful:—

(*a*) **Ain't.**—There is no such word as *ain't* in the English language; yet we often hear it used for *am not, is not, are not.* Since no such word exists, it ought not to be used even in talking, much less in writing.

He *ain't* going to be beaten. (Change to *is not.*)
I *ain't* feeling well to-day. (Change to *am not.*)
They *ain't* of any use. (Change to *are not.*)

(*b*) **Didn't ought.**—This is very bad English; yet we often hear it among certain classes. *Did* is a Past tense, and *ought* is a Past tense. Two Past tenses cannot be put together in this way. For *did not ought* or *didn't ought* say simply *ought not*, and if you wish to express Past time, change the Present Infinitive following into the Past Infinitive:—

He *didn't ought to say* that. (Wrong.)
{ He *ought not to have said* that. (*Past time.*)
{ He *ought not to say* that. (*Present time.*)

(*c*) **Don't.**—This is a contraction of *do not.* We may therefore say (*i.e.* in talking, not in writing), I *don't, you don't, we don't*, or *they don't.* But we cannot say *he don't, she don't*, or *it don't*, because *he, she*, or *it* (3rd person Singular) must be followed by *does* (3rd person Singular).

He *don't* know. (Change to *does not.*)
It *don't* matter. (Change to *does not.*)

Note.—The contractions *won't, can't, shan't* for *will not, cannot*, and *shall not* respectively can be used (in all numbers and both persons) in conversation, but not in written composition.

Exercise on § 11. (To be done orally and at sight.)

Correct any mistakes that you find in the following:—

1. He don't mind being told when he is in the wrong.
2. I ain't in any hurry this morning; so keep your seat.
3. Four weeks' pay is now due to me; he don't pay in time.
4. He didn't ought to keep me waiting for four weeks.
5. He is a kind of man who don't know his own mind.
6. Why don't he go away? Every one is scolding him.
7. It don't matter how often you are spoken to; you don't care.

8. He ain't going to be so foolish again; pardon him this time.

9. He can't understand you, and, what is more, he don't try.

10. She didn't ought to go away: it ain't right of her.

11. The cow don't belong to us; so you can take her away.

12. I shan't go on with this work, if he don't pay me.

13. I can't see any reason why he don't like my work.

14. We don't mind this noise, and he don't mind it either.

15. It ain't of any use talking to you; you don't care.

16. Don't go on finding fault; you didn't ought to do so.

17. I don't wish to see him; and he don't wish to see me.

18. Ain't you going out to-day? It don't rain now.

19. Don't you see that horse? It don't run so fast as that every day

20. We didn't ought to have laughed: he don't like it.

21. There ain't no such thing as a mountain in this country.

22. The money ain't in the bank now: I took it out.

12. Imperative Mood.—When the verb is negative, *i.e.* when it prohibits or forbids something, we use the Auxiliary "*do*," as in the present tense Indicative (§ 9):—

Imperative.	*Prohibitive.*
Come here.	*Do not* or *don't* come here.

Note.—In the Tudor period, as we see from the language of the Bible, the Auxiliary *do* was not used for the purpose of prohibition:—

Judge not, that ye be not judged.—*Matt.* vii.

Exercise on § 12. (To be done orally and at sight.)

Convert the main verb in each of the following sentences from Imperative to Prohibitive or vice versâ, *and make any change of language in the rest of the sentence that may be required by the sense :—*

1. Send the book over to my house, as I cannot call for it.
2. In building a house don't use any but the best materials.
3. Do not work overtime, unless you are paid extra for it.
4. Give me some help, if you can spare a little time.
5. As I am able to carry the parcel, do not send it by a porter.
6. In choosing a horse do not trust to your own judgment, unless you are a very experienced judge.
7. Paint the door of the house green, if you prefer it.
8. Do not come here this evening, if you are not feeling better.
9. Read that book : it will repay perusal.
10. Do not do unto others what you would not like that others should do unto you.
11. Treat a dumb animal in such a way as you would like to be treated yourself.
12. Unless the air is warm enough, do not go out into the open.

SECTION 3.—NOMINATIVE AND OBJECTIVE CASES.

13. Nominative.—All nouns have the same form for the Nominative and the Objective cases ; but most of the pronouns have one form for the Nominative and another for the Objective ; as *I, me ; he, him ; she, her ; we, us ; they, them ; who, whom ; thou, thee* (rarely used).

The Nominative form of the pronoun must be used (*a*) when the pronoun is the Subject of a verb, or (*b*) when it is placed after the verb *is* or *was* :—

(*a*) *He* will come. This is the man *who* spoke.
(*b*) It is *I* (not *me*). That is *he* (not *him*).

Exercise on § 13. (To be done orally and at sight.)

Correct any mistakes that you find in the following:—

1. Us three will play you four, and beat you, I expect.
2. It was me who wrote that letter, not him.
3. Her and Mrs. J. were expected here to-day.
4. I have no doubt at all that it was her who spoke.
5. Him and his father were both taken ill that day.
6. Them's the lazy fellows that we have to pay for.
7. Whom do men say that I am?
8. I would not do such a thing as that if I were him.
9. I was quite certain that it could not be her.
10. Was it me that you were speaking to, or was it him?
11. Them that say such things ought not to be believed.
12. Tom, William, and me went out for a ramble.
13. I have a son, whom I intend shall learn Greek.
14. My brother and me will get home by four o'clock.
15. I knew it was her fault all the time; but her won't confess.
16. Her father and me will soon find out where she is.
17. Who is that knocking at the door? Me, sir.
18. Him and me were playing at marbles outside the school door.
19. Them that are idle and mischievous are not wanted here.
20. May Robert and me go out for a walk by ourselves?
21. Us two soon began to be tired of having nothing to do.
22. Who made that noise? Not him, sir, but me.
23. Were you there, or was it him that I saw?
24. Whom do you suppose called on me yesterday?

14. Objective.—The Objective form of the pronoun must be used—(*a*) when the pronoun is the Object of a Transitive verb; (*b*) when it is the Object of a Preposition; (*c*) when it is placed after the verb "*to be*," and this Infinitive is preceded by a Transitive verb with its Object; (*d*) when it is placed after the adjectives "*like*," "*unlike*," or "*near*":—

(*a*) I will bring *him*. *Whom* are you expecting?
(*b*) I have great faith in *them*. In *whom* do you trust?
(*c*) That man is so like Tom that I took it to be *him*.
(*d*) The portrait you have painted is very like *him*.

Exercise on § 14. (To be done orally and at sight.)

Correct any mistakes that you find in the following:—

1. Who were you speaking to just now, and what did you say?
2. Between you and I, the boy that stands there is a dunce.
3. There's quite enough room in this carriage for you and I.
4. He is a clever man, and I don't know who he is like.
5. He and they we know to be quite honest and truthful.
6. They asked my friend and I to call upon them to-day.
7. He or she that is idle send out of the class.
8. Not a man in the room can swim or dive like he.
9. Will you take mother and I out with you to-day?
10. Who did you think him to be after all?
11. I have bought some ripe apples for William and she.
12. He that spilt this ink I shall fine sixpence.
13. Let you and I see what we can do in this game.
14. I understood it to be he all the time.
15. Let them and we enter into partnership.
16. Take care to let my friend and I know when to come.
17. Remember who you are speaking to: take care what you say.
18. Who did you expect to see at this time of day?
19. He hurt my sister and I very much, that he did.
20. Who did you refer to, when you made that remark?
21. He defeated we three, but us beat him in return.

22. He could not have done that without the help of mother and I.

23. Does a man like he expect to do well in the world?

24. They called I a dunce, because I said "I" for "me."

25. It is you that want protection, not me.

15. From Active to Passive Voice.—When the verb of a sentence is changed from the Active voice to the Passive, what was the Object of the Active verb becomes the Subject of the Passive. The change from Object to Subject involves a change of case from Objective to Nominative:—

Active.—A bull attacked my brother and *me.*

Passive.—My brother and *I* were attacked by a bull.

Exercise on § 15. (To be done orally and at sight.)

Change the voices of the verbs in the following sentences:—

1. I was much hurt by his voice and manner.
2. We all expected his return, but we were disappointed.
3. If a cat may look at a king, it may look at me too.
4. Should he find me at home, I would not receive him.
5. The policeman caught him asleep behind a hedge.
6. The city welcomed them back on their return from the battlefield.
7. The master punished him for speaking in class.
8. Will not a sense of duty persuade him to work better?
9. We raised many objections to the plan that he proposed.
10. The meeting called upon me to give my reasons.
11. The general ordered them to present guns and fire.
12. He requested me to give him the post, but I did not grant his request.
13. I knew him by his voice, when he spoke to me in the dark.

14. A random shot struck him on horseback and threw him.

15. As she had been warned more than once, it was not likely that she would be forgiven this time by the mistress.

16. The new rule lately issued has injured us in various ways.

17. My brother, much against my will, forced me to sign this bond.

18. As they did not pay the rent, he ordered them to leave at once.

19. Oh, woodman, spare that tree,
Touch not a single bough;
In youth it sheltered me,
And I'll protect it now.

20. He was struck by lightning, as he sat under a tree.

21. The language that he used quite shocked me.

22. I am the wearer, and I know best where the shoe pinches.

23. Who rang that bell? Not I, sir,—certainly not I.

24. Whom did they blame for that unfortunate accident?

25. I beheld a sight which pleased and interested me much.

26. The health and happiness of the child did not concern him much.

27. Whom did he invite to attend the meeting?

28. The sight of that event filled both of us with horror.

16. Case of Pronoun after "than" or "as."—After the conjunction *than* or *as*, the noun or pronoun following is sometimes the only word expressed:—

(*a*) He likes you better than *me*.
(*b*) He likes you better than *I*.

Which is right—*me* or *I*? Both are right, but the two sentences do not mean the same thing. To find out in which case the pronoun should be, ask yourself what the sentence is intended to mean, and then repeat the verb that has been mentioned already in the preceding clause:—

(*a*) He likes you better than (he likes) *me*.
(*b*) He likes you better than *I* (like you).

In (*a*) the pronoun *me* is in the Objective case, because it is the Object of the unexpressed Transitive verb "likes," which is understood and carried forward from the previous sentence. In (*b*) the pronoun "I" is in the Nominative case, because it is the Subject of the unexpressed Transitive verb "like," understood and carried forward from the previous sentence.

(*c*) He likes you as much as (he likes) *me*.
(*d*) He likes you as much as *I* (like you).

Here, as before, the case of the pronoun placed after *as* depends upon whether the pronoun is meant to be the Object or the Subject of the missing verb.

(*e*) He is taller than *me*. He is as tall as *me*.

Here *me* should be changed to *I* in both sentences, because in both the missing verb is *am*. We cannot say, "He is taller than *me am*," or "He is as tall as *me am*." The *me* must therefore be changed to *I*, and made the Subject of the verb "am."

Exercises on § 16. (To be done orally and at sight.)

(*a*) *Supply the missing verb or verbs in the following sentences without altering the case of the pronoun coming after "than" or "as":—*

1. He is as clever as I, but not so clever as Tom.
2. I have not written so much or so clearly as he.
3. He mastered the drift of the subject more thoroughly than I.
4. Tom has seen that man quite as often as me.
5. Tom has seen that man quite as often as I.
6. They take as much pleasure in work as he in idleness.
7. The dog barks more fiercely at you than at them.
8. The matron of the house knows me better than him.

9. The matron of the house knows me better than he.

10. The writer understood the subject better than they.

11. He is better off than I in money, but I am better off than he in knowing how to spend it.

12. He worked harder than you, when he was preparing for his examination.

13. None are so blind as they who will not see.

14. He is as great an offender as William himself.

15. This workman is not so industrious as some of the others.

16. So brave a man as he was never seen before.

17. The mother likes to be admired as much as he.

18. My friends are not so numerous, but they are quite as true as yours.

19. No one can be more astonished than I at this news.

20. That book impressed me more than him.

21. He is not welcomed more cordially than any other guest.

22. Few men have been more witty than Dickens.

23. In one lesson I made more faults than he in two.

24. He is more true to his friends than they to him.

(*b*) *Correct any mistakes that you find in the following, and supply the missing verbs:—*

1. You had quite as good a chance of success as me.

2. A. and B. are better off than us in everything.

3. My partners have gained more than me by this plan.

4. Though her brother has studied more books than her, he has not so much common-sense as her in daily life.

5. He rides better than her, but she sings better than him.

6. The nations not so blessed as thee
   Must in their turn to tyrants fall.—THOMSON.

7. That author wrote a much better book than him.

8. He is richer than me in cash, but not in reputation.

9. None are so deaf as them that refuse to hear.

10. Very few persons spoke so well as him at the meeting.

11. I never before saw any girl so pretty as her.

12. He was more averse than me to the study of books.

13. He is more convinced than me of the truth of that saying.

14. No one is more to be pitied than him for what has happened.

15. He was more hardly used than us; so we can't complain.

16. Though she is only ten years old, she can run quicker than him or me.

SECTION 4.—PERSONAL AND DEMONSTRATIVE PRONOUNS.

17. Position of Personal pronoun.—In speaking of oneself and others the pronoun "*I*" should be mentioned last:—

James and I had a long walk. (Right.)
I and James had a long walk. (Wrong.)

There is no rule about the position of "*you.*" It is rather more common, however, to mention the "*you*" first:—

You and James must be back by four o'clock.

Exercises on § 17. (To be done orally and at sight.)

(*a*) *Join the following pairs of sentences into one, mentioning the verb only once, and putting the two pronouns in their proper order*:—

1. I can go to-morrow. You can go to-morrow.
2. I rowed the boat. The boatman rowed the boat.
3. You must work harder. James must work harder.
4. You have been invited. Your father has been invited.
5. He saw the horse kick. I saw the horse kick.
6. The guests were glad of that. We were glad of that.
7. I was not afraid. The boatman was not afraid.
8. The noise alarmed us. The noise alarmed him.
9. The music delighted me. The music delighted you.

(*b*) *Correct any mistakes of order, number, or case that you find in the following sentences :—*

1. Them and me had a great deal of fun that day.
2. Me and my sister are much pleased with that song.
3. I hope you will invite my sister and I again.
4. Who have been invited? William and us.
5. Us and the three boys went out to fly the kite.
6. Me and Smith will play James and he.
7. Them who made that noise was I and James.
8. This heavy road has tired out my pony and I.
9. It is now fine; me and my sister want to go out.

18. Demonstrative pronouns.—To avoid repeating a noun (which does not sound well), we use the Demonstrative pronouns, *that* or *those.* The pronoun so used must be of the same number as the noun that it stands for :—

The *climate* of England is cooler than *that* (=the climate) of India. (Singular.)

The *fish* of the sea are larger than *those* (=the fish) of rivers. (Plural.)

If the noun going before is preceded by the Indefinite article, it must be followed by the Indefinite Demonstrative *one* :—

A box made of wood is lighter than *one* (=a box) made of iron.

Exercise on § 18. (To be done orally and at sight.)

Insert the proper pronoun in the places left blank :—

1. A house built of brick lasts longer than —— built of wood.
2. The people of England are more hardy than —— of Spain.
3. The voice of a woman is softer than —— of a man.
4. The cattle of this county are larger than —— of Yorkshire.

5. The men of Rome were more warlike than —— of Athens.

6. The sting of a wasp gives less pain than —— of a hornet.

7. The air of hills is cooler than —— of lowlands.

8. The horns of these oxen are less crooked than —— of stags.

9. The ceiling of my room is higher than —— of yours.

10. I prefer your singing to —— of your sister.

11. I like books on science better than —— on language.

12. A glass of plain water will suit you better than —— of wine.

19. Precautions.—There are two common errors to be guarded against:—

(*a*) *Them* must not be placed before a noun, in the place of *these* or *those*:—

Them things are not wanted. (Say *these* or *those*.)

(*b*) *Here* should not be placed after *this* or *these*; and *there* should not be placed after *that* or *these*. Neither of these adverbs adds anything to the sense.

This *here* thorn gives me much pain. (Omit *here*.)
That *there* bull is dangerous. (Omit *there*.)

Exercise on § 19. (To be done orally and at sight.)

Correct any mistakes that you find in the following:—

1. Send them boys over here; it is their turn now.
2. Them there words have been badly spelt.
3. This here box was very nearly lost on the way.
4. I cannot allow him to speak to me in that there way.
5. Them tools will be lost, if you leave them lying about.
6. I have engaged this here man for the next three days.
7. We lived in that there old house for four years.
8. This flower looks much prettier than that there.

9. I am tired of hearing them songs day after day.

10. These here apples are much sweeter than those there pears.

11. Them trees have more fruit this year than last.

12. Them's the men who helped to build that there house.

13. I like the flower of a rose, but I don't like them thorns.

14. Them there strawberries are very nearly fit to pick.

15. This here boy is always talking instead of learning.

CHAPTER II.—FORMATION OF SIMPLE SENTENCES.

20. What a Simple Sentence is.—When a Subject and a Verb are so combined as to make a complete sense, the combination is called a **Sentence.**

The sentence is called **Simple** (that is, *Single*) when it contains only *one* Finite verb. (On the meaning of "Finite verb," see § 1, *Note* 1.)

(1) James went. (2) Who did this? (3) Go (thou or you).

In (1) the sentence expresses a fact or makes a statement. In (2) the sentence asks a question. In (3) the sentence expresses an order (the Subject "thou" or "you" being understood). Each of them, whatever its form or purport may be, makes a complete sense; and therefore each of them is a sentence.

21. Phrase.—When two or more words are so combined as to make sense, but not a *complete* sense, the combination is not a sentence, but a **Phrase**:—

(1) Up a steep hill. (2) A frisky horse. (3) Among when see black.

The words in (1) make sense as far as they go. But there is neither a verb nor a subject in them, and therefore they do not make a sentence,—only a phrase. The words in (2) make sense as far as they go; but, as before, the result is only a phrase. The words in (3) do not give any sense whatever. The combination is sheer nonsense. So they do not make even a phrase, much less a sentence.

Exercise on §§ 20, 21. (To be done orally and at sight.)

In the following examples say which are sentences and which are phrases. In every sentence pick out the Subject and Finite verb:—

1. The horse kicks.
2. Stop.
3. Decidedly clever.
4. Well up to date.
5. You laughed.
6. Inside the house.
7. Men work.
8. Women knit.
9. A beautiful singer.
10. Sit down.
11. On the top.
12. At six o'clock.
13. John has come.
14. Two weeks ago.
15. Boys play.
16. Twice a day.
17. Through the air.
18. Fire burns.
19. Below the surface.
20. On board ship.
21. The snake crawls.
22. It is raining.
23. Wait a little.
24. The cat mews.
25. Along the bank.
26. To and fro.
27. Wolves howl.
28. Upside down.
29. How are you?
30. Down the stream.
31. Time flies.
32. In a boat.
33. Hard at work.

22. Subject and Predicate.—Every sentence, whatever its length may happen to be, consists of two main parts.

The first part (the name of the person or thing spoken of) is called the **Subject.** This has been described already. A Subject may be expressed in many different forms, but the most common form is that of a noun or pronoun in the Nominative case.

The second part (what is said about the person or thing) is called the **Predicate.** The Predicate is either a Finite verb or it contains one.

When the sentence is very short, consisting of only two words, as "rain fell," the division into Subject and Predicate is very simple: *rain* is the Subject or Nominative, and *fell* is the Predicate or Finite verb. It will be afterwards seen that the longest sentence can be divided into the same two parts as the shortest.

Exercises on § 22. (To be done orally and at sight.)

(*a*) *Supply a Subject (some noun or pronoun in the Nominative case) to each Predicate or Finite verb given below:—*

1. — speaks.
2. — have spoken.
3. — burns.
4. — flashes.
5. — goes away.
6. — has gone.
7. — have gone.
8. — floats.
9. — kicks.
10. — kick.
11. — neighed.
12. — falls.
13. — fall.
14. — shouted.
15. — plays.
16. — works.
17. — am working.
18. — are working.
19. — flows.
20. — remain.
21. — grazes.
22. — has stood.
23. — stand.
24. — come.
25. — am coming.
26. — howl.
27. — roar.
28. — sleeps.
29. — weeps.
30. — bark.
31. — laughed.
32. — laughs.
33. — fights.
34. — were laughing.
35. — shines.
36. — shone.
37. — rises.
38. — swim.
39. — has swum.
40. — is dawning.
41. — floats.
42. — departs.
43. — run.
44. — runs.
45. — crawl.
46. — hiss.
47. — growls.
48. — buzz.
49. — blows.
50. — stings.
51. — sings.
52. — talk.
53. — chatter.
54. — is jumping.
55. — cries.

(*b*) *Supply a Predicate or Finite verb to each Subject:—*

1. A boy —
2. Boys
3. A fish —
4. Fish —
5. I —
6. He —
7. We —
8. A horse —
9. Horses —
10. A wasp —
11. The girl —
12. A monkey —
13. A house —
14. Houses —
15. A lion —
16. The lions —
17. The sun —
18. The day —
19. The workman —
20. The workmen —
21. Rain —
22. Soldiers —
23. Watchman —
24. Watchmen —
25. A bee —
26. Dogs —
27. A cat —
28. Mice —
29. Some one —
30. Who —
31. They —
32. The wind —
33. The wolf —
34. Wolves —
35. The porter —
36. Fire —
37. The moon —
38. The snake —
39. Cows —
40. A snake —
41. A ploughman —
42. The boat —
43. A boatman—
44. Ships —
45. The river —
46. Mother —
47. Lightning —
48. Grass —
49. Boatmen —
50. The ox —
51. The tower —
52. A storm —
53. Teeth —

23. Verb and Object.—Sometimes the Predicate consists of a verb only, as "James *went*," "Rain *fell*." In such sentences the verb is Intransitive; see the Examples given in § 22 (*a*).

But if the verb is Transitive, that is, if it requires some **Object** to be placed after it in order to make the sense complete, then the verb and the object together make up the Predicate, as shown in the following form :—

I. SUBJECT.	II. PREDICATE.	
	Finite verb.	Object.
Bees	gather	honey.
James	has lost	his kite.
Rain	moistens	the ground.
He	is reading	a book.

Exercises on § 23. (To be done orally and at sight.)

(*a*) *Supply an Object to the Finite verb of each sentence* :—

1. The boatman has received ——. 2. Soldiers defend ——. 3. A snake has bitten ——. 4. Mother has cooked ——. 5. I have written ——. 6. Why did you laugh at ——? 7. The boys have finished ——. 8. He is riding ——. 9. The porter will carry ——. 10. Lightning struck ——. 11. A messenger has brought ——. 12. The monkey frightened ——. 13. The watchman protects ——. 14. The girl has plucked ——. 15. How did you find out ——? 16. When did you see ——? 17. Wolves attacked ——. 18. The sun will ripen ——. 19. Ploughmen till ——. 20. The hunter has caught ——. 21. The gardener is planting ——. 22. The bird has built ——. 23. The cow gives ——. 24. We dislike ——. 25. The dog pursued ——. 26. Authors write ——. 27. The river overflows ——. 28. The horse kicked ——. 29. Night succeeds ——, and day succeeds ——. 30. Give me ——.

(*b*) *Supply a Subject to the Finite verb of each sentence* :—

1. —— brought a message. 2. —— shot a wolf. 3. —— have plucked a rose. 4. —— climbs the trees. 5. —— boils the kettle. 6. —— rides a horse. 7. ——

is sowing seeds. 8. —— built a house. 9. —— plough the field. 10. —— kill mice. 11. —— struck the dog. 12. —— hung up his coat. 13. —— attacked the enemy. 14. —— gives light. 15. —— found out the secret. 16. —— made a coat. 17. —— drew the cart. 18. —— overflowed its banks. 19. —— swept the room. 20. —— expects a prize. 21. —— cut down the tree. 22. —— made a box. 23. —— will catch the thief. 24. —— found out his mistake. 25. —— pardoned the offender. 26. —— heard a report. 27. —— dig the ground. 28. —— eat hay. 29. —— sang a song. 30. —— kicked his rider.

(*c*) *Supply a Finite verb in the Present tense to each sentence :—*

1. The gardener —— seeds. 2. The girl —— a flower. 3. The workman —— his work. 4. He —— a prize. 5. A snake —— the dog. 6. Father —— a horse. 7. The messenger —— his pay. 8. The watchman —— the tower. 9. The tailor —— a coat. 10. The wolf —— the sheep. 11. He —— his sister. 12. The carpenter —— a door. 13. The moon —— light. 14. The woodman —— an axe. 15. The thieves —— a watch. 16. Oxen —— grass. 17. Father —— a letter. 18. The bird —— a nest. 19. Trees —— a shade. 20. The sun —— the ground. 21. The policeman —— the thief. 22. The hounds —— the hare. 23. A cobbler —— shoes. 24. The messenger —— news. 25. The monkey —— the child. 26. The dog —— the cat. 27. The smith —— a kettle. 28. The wind —— the tree. 29. The river —— its banks.

24. How longer Sentences are subdivided.—We have seen thus far that there are three kinds of words on which the structure of a Simple sentence (if the verb is Transitive) depends :—

A. The Nominative (or its equivalent) ;
B. The Finite verb ;
C. The Object of the verb.

But it very often happens that A, B, C are each accompanied by certain other words, which, though they are not essential to the structure of the sentence, add much to its meaning. These may be called—

(*a*) Modifications[1] of the Nominative;
(*b*) Modifications of the Finite verb;
(*c*) Modifications of the Object.

We may take as an example the following sentence:—

A hungry fox, prowling about in search of food, was eagerly watching some ripe grapes hanging from a wall.

The parts of this sentence may be shown in tabular form as follows:—

I. Subject.		II. Predicate.			
Nominative. A	Modification of Nominative. a	Finite Verb. B	Modification of Finite Verb. b	Object. C	Modification of Object. c
A[2] fox	hungry, prowling about in search of food,	was watching	eagerly	grapes	some ripe hanging from a wall.

25. Oral Analysis of Sentences.—To enable the student to acquire facility in understanding the differ-

[1] These are called "Modifications," because they modify or alter the meaning of the Nominative, the meaning of the Verb, or the meaning of the Object. Sometimes they are called "Adjuncts," because they consist of words which are *added* to the Nominative, the Verb, or the Object. The words added to the Nominative or to the Object are sometimes called the "Enlargement," and those added to the Verb are sometimes called the "Extension." "Enlargement" and "Extension," however, mean the same thing.

[2] Properly speaking, an article, Definite or Indefinite, is a modification of a Noun, and in the analysis of sentences it is so treated. For purposes of composition, however, it is more convenient to place the article in the same column with its noun.

ent parts of a sentence and in answering questions respecting each part of the sentence in turn, we recommend some such form as the following. (It will, of course, be understood that when there is nothing in the sentence corresponding to some of the letters such as *a*, *b*, *C*, *c*, no question can be asked respecting these.)

(1) A hungry fox, prowling about in search of food, was eagerly watching some ripe grapes hanging from a wall.

	Teacher.	*Student.*
Nominative	A. What was watching the grapes?	A fox.
Mod. Nom.	*a.* What more about the fox?	It was hungry, prowling about in search of food.
Fin. Verb	B. What was the fox doing?	It was watching some grapes.
Mod. Fin. V.	*b.* What more about the watching?	It was watching them eagerly.
Object	C. What things was the fox watching?	Grapes.
Mod. Object	*c.* What more about the grapes?	They were ripe grapes, hanging from a wall.

(2) In autumn most trees shed their dead leaves.

	Teacher.	*Student.*
Nominative	A. What things shed their leaves?	Trees.
Mod. Nom.	*a.* What more about the trees?	Most trees do this.
Fin. Verb.	B. What do the trees do?	They shed their leaves.
Mod. Fin. V.	*b.* What more about the shedding?	They shed them in autumn.
Object	C. What do the trees shed?	Their leaves.
Mod. Object	*c.* What more about the leaves?	The leaves are dead.

Exercise on § 25.

Let the teacher question each student in turn on the method shown above:—

1. Wider knowledge will no doubt remove false ideas.
2. The king's messenger brought good news to the city.
3. A sharp frost would destroy those beautiful buds in one night.

4. A spreading oak affords a cool and pleasant shade to the weary and foot-sore traveller.

5. The cobbler living next door mends our shoes very well.

6. That troublesome smith has not yet repaired the leaking kettle.

7. The moon now rising will give a cool and soft light for some hours at least of the night.

8. The sun of spring and summer brings flowers into bloom.

9. The cold of winter hardens the surface of the earth with frost.

10. Wise men use the passing hour to some purpose.

11. A thoughtful person learns many useful things from experience.

12. Book-learning without common-sense brings no profit to any one.

13. True merit brings out a good result with very little noise.

14. The senior boy of the class will write a short letter to-morrow on the subject of the recent trip.

15. Instead of waiting till to-morrow, the boy referred to wrote that letter to-day.

16. The residents of hot countries chiefly wear clothes made of cotton.

17. The brave shepherd drove the wolf out of the field.

18. He received with a grateful heart a reward proportionate to his deserts.

19. The ship, having struck on the rocks, sank with all its cargo and passengers on board.

20. The horse, fatigued by the journey and lame of one foot, fell on the road.

21. A good book on the subject of China is much wanted at the present time.

22. Watching his chance, he seized the ferocious dog by the collar.

23. The above-named person came punctually to the hour.

24. A man full of words will not prosper on the earth.

25. A bleak and blustering wind, suddenly springing up, met us on the way towards Dover.

26. The clouds coming from the west have given a cool and refreshing shower.

27. The last news from China gave genuine and unmixed satisfaction.

28. The work of the campaign was carried out effectively by the general.

29. A stitch in time saves nine.

30. The romances of Sir Walter Scott always give the greatest pleasure.

31. A prudent man learns by degrees the proper time to speak or act.

32. Every student kept his right place in the master's presence.

33. A storm of thunder and lightning seriously impeded the progress of the travellers.

34. The workmen engaged for this job certainly require more time.

35. Your son for some time past has shown decided improvement in almost all his studies.

36. All farmers expect fine weather at this season.

37. In the long run industry and perseverance have the reward due to them.

38. The book just named will no doubt please any man of clear understanding.

39. The demolition of the bridge averted for a time the approach of the enemy.

40. That ship riding at anchor in the harbour astonishes me more and more with its bulk.

41. A hard-working labourer sometimes receives but a poor return for all his industry.

42. The Director of the firm helped forward the new project with much zeal and energy.

43. The Athenian judges in condemning Socrates to death committed a great crime.

44. He kept his promised engagement to-day at four o'clock.

45. The lecturer in the Town Hall pleased the audience very much with his amusing anecdotes.

46. St. Paul claimed the rights of a Roman citizen in his defence.

26. How the Nominative or the Object can be modified.—There are many different ways in which the Nominative (that is, the Subject of a sentence, whenever the Subject is expressed by a noun or pronoun) can be modified. Six different ways are shown in the examples given below. These all apply to the Object also, if the sentence has one. All such enlargements of a noun or pronoun are expressed either by an adjective or by some word or phrase that does the work of an adjective.

(*a*) **Adjective.**	A *just* man deserves to prosper. A *just and industrious* man deserves to prosper. A man *full*-of-words shall not prosper.
(*b*) **Participle.**	A *fertilising* shower fell to-day. A shower *fertilising*-the-earth fell to-day. *Having completed*-his-work he went away. *Fatigued*-with-his-journey he rested a little.
(*c*) **Possessive Noun or Pronoun.**	*William's* teacher has come. *Our* teacher has come.
(*d*) **Infinitive.**	Water *to drink* is scarce in this place. (Trans. verb.) He wants a chair *to sit* on. (Intrans. verb.)
(*e*) **Noun or Gerund used as Adjective.**	The *village* school reopens to-day. (Noun.) *Drinking* water is scarce in this place. (Gerund.)

(*f*) **Prep. with Object.**—A man *of honour* can be trusted.

Note on (*d*).—When the verb is Intransitive, as *to sit*, it must be followed by a Preposition, as *to sit on*. The sentence, if it were fully expressed, would be, "He wants a chair to sit on it." Though the *it* is not expressed, the preposition must not be left out.

Exercises on § 26. (To be done orally and at sight.)

(*a*) *Modify the Nominative or the Object or both after the manner shown in* (*a*), *using any adjectives that make good sense.*—

1. A —— wind was blowing all yesterday; it blew down —— trees. 2. A —— letter reached us to-day; it gave us —— pleasure. 3. The —— student has gained a —— prize. 4. A —— oak tree gives a —— shade. 5. The —— child has just gone to sleep. 6. A —— fire was burning: it warmed the —— room. 7. A —— friend gives —— advice. 8. The —— hermit occupied a —— hut. 9. I have —— pleasure in accepting —— invitation. 10. I shall have —— pleasure in dining with you. 11. The —— traveller enjoyed —— sleep. 12. A —— robber frequents —— road. 13. A —— fog has arisen. 14. A —— frost has set in. 15. The —— garden has yielded —— fruit. 16. A —— breeze on a hot day is refreshing. 17. A —— storm upset the —— boat. 18. A —— smell and —— drainage do —— injury to one's health. 19. A —— fire on a cold day is very cheerful. 20. A —— shower after all this drought would do —— good. 21. —— heart never won a —— lady. 22. He showed —— energy all his life.

(*b*) *Modify the Nominative after the manner shown in* (*b*); *and modify the Object in that or any other way*:—

1. A box —— has just been delivered. 2. The thief —— was locked up. 3. A —— rain has been falling all day. 4. The —— stag attacked at last the dogs ——. 5. The —— flowers need a —— watering. 6. A fall of rain will refresh the —— crops. 7. A —— bat will not be fit to play with. 8. His —— boots make a —— noise. 9. Let —— dogs lie. 10. Did any one —— meet you? 11. The —— sun makes the birds begin to sing. 12. —— we listened to the birds ——. 13. —— he felt tired. 14. The news —— made every one feel happy.

(*c*) *Modify the Nominative by using Possessives* (*the noun or pronoun being given in brackets*) *after the manner shown in* (*c*). *Modify the Object in that or any of the other ways shown in* § 26, *using any words that make good sense :—*

1. (We) house has a roof. 2. (Dog) kennel requires paint. 3. (You) invitation deserves (I) best thanks. 4. (Ladies) dresses looked very handsome. 5. The result did not equal (we) expectations. 6. (She) singing delighted the company. 7. He must accept (judge) decision. 8. The flood has overflowed (river) banks. 9. (Bride) veil was much admired. 10. Every one must mind (he) business.

(*d*) *Modify the Nominative or the Object after the manner shown in* (*d*) :—

1. Being very thirsty, we want some water ——. 2. Feeling tired, I was glad to find a bed ——. 3. I have no money ——. 4. A workman must have tools ——. 5. A house —— could not be found in that street. 6. I have found an interesting book ——. 7. She has no piano ——. 8. I have no paper ——. 9. There is no clock or watch ——. 10. He had two sons and three daughters ——. 11. A flock of sheep needs a shepherd ——. 12. His health is bad; he wants some medicine ——. 13. A dog —— will add much to his safety. 14. You must get a porter ——.

(*e*) *Modify the Nominative or the Object after the manner shown in* (*e*) :—

1. The —— season has now set in. 2. I must buy a new —— stick. 3. We get —— water from this well. 4. The —— clock loses time. 5. We must get some —— tools. 6. The —— garden is looking very pretty. 7. You cannot part your hair well without the help of a —— glass. 8. I should like to have a swim; but there is no —— place here. 9. I cannot manage this horse without a —— whip. 10. Be so good as to fasten up this envelope with some —— wax. 11. The —— post will show us the way. 12. This brook can be crossed by —— stones. 13. He had a fine —— park in front of his house. 14. I cannot mend your pencil properly without a —— knife.

15. To correct that bill I referred to my —— book. 16. The —— prince in England is called the Prince of Wales.

(*f*) *Modify the Nominative or the Object after the manner shown in* (*f*):—

1. A friend —— is a friend indeed. 2. I prefer a man —— to a man ——. 3. A cry —— was heard from the boat. 4. A pack —— was brought into the hunting-field. 5. The Prince —— is heir to the English throne. 6. Walking —— is good for health. 7. A dive —— refreshed him. 8. A word —— might have prevented further mischief. 9. The Book —— has been ascribed to King Solomon. 10. A forest —— surrounds the castle. 11. A hedge —— looks beautiful in summer. 12. She wore a wreath ——. 13. A rest —— did us all much good. 14. The gardener brought in a good supply ——.

27. How the Finite verb can be modified.—There are many different ways in which the Finite verb of a Simple sentence can be modified. The principal ones are given below. All such extensions of the Finite verb have reference to time, or place, or manner, or cause, or motive, or degree, or number, or state; and are expressed either by an adverb or by some phrase that does the work of an adverb.

(*a*) **Adverb.**	He slept *soundly* and *uninterruptedly*.
(*b*) **Adverbial phrase.**	He slept *for six hours*. We shall do better *next time*.
(*c*) **Infinitive.**	He came *to see*-the-horse. The horse was taken to the farrier *to be shod*.
(*d*) **Absolute phrase.**	*Dinner being finished*, they left the room. We all set off, *he remaining behind*.

Note on (*d*).—Observe that when a pronoun is used in the absolute construction, it is in the Nominative case; as "*he* remaining behind."

Exercises on § 27. (To be done orally and at sight.)

(*a*) *Modify the Finite verb after the manner shown in* (*a*):—

1. He walks ——. 2. He will —— return. 3. Let us go out ——. 4. He would —— do such a thing as that. 5. He read the book ——. 6. He listened ——. 7. The lad was punished ——. 8. They warned him ——. 9. The gardener worked ——. 10. He was —— paid. 11. The mouse peeped —— out of its hole. 12. He is —— improving. 13. John will return ——. 14. Mistakes are —— made by careless persons. 15. The poor girl was crying ——. 16. The bell is tolling —— for the man who has —— died. 17. The boat rides —— before the wind. 18. The child has —— been ill with a cough. 19. The child coughs ——. 20. The birds are singing —— all day. 21. The tide is —— rising. 22. The sun is —— going down.

(*b*) *Modify the Finite verb after the manner shown in* (*b*) :—

1. He walked ——. 2. The apple fell ——. 3. I am suffering ——. 4. The wind is blowing ——. 5. I shall get there ——. 6. The cows are lying ——. 7. He smiled ——. 8. They pelted the poor creature ——. 9. A fox is hunted ——. 10. Every one trembled ——. 11. The patient lay awake ——. 12. The mouse was caught ——. 13. A mouse hides ——. 14. Let us take a stroll ——. 15. No one can see his way ——. 16. A house should not be built ——. 17. The attack was directed ——. 18. A true friend will take trouble ——. 19. He makes mistakes ——. 20. We cannot do this ——. 21. We hope to do better ——. 22. They were walking ——.

(*c*) *Modify the Finite verb after the manner shown in* (*c*) :—

Note.—This form of extension usually expresses the motive or purpose for which anything is done. So in filling up the blank, think of some purpose for which the action expressed by the Finite verb is likely to be done.

1. The thieves have entered the house ——. 2. The messenger came ——. 3. We shall leave home ——. 4.

The gardener has come ——. 5. A fire was lighted ——. 6. He bought a water-can ——. 7. He engaged a groom ——. 8. Send for a carpenter ——. 9. Send for a mason ——. 10. Send for a plumber ——. 11. Stop here a little ——. 12. He hired a boat ——. 13. The coat was given to the tailor ——. 14. The student worked hard ——. 15. He went to the grocer ——. 16. She went to the draper ——. 17. The bell was rung ——. 18. The patient went to the hospital ——. 19. A wolf came into the field ——.

(*d*) *Modify the Finite verb after the manner shown in* (*d*): —

Note.—The verb to be used absolutely with noun or pronoun is given in brackets.

1. (The enemy, defeat), the army left the field. 2. All this was said (you, I, listen). 3. (The tide, recede), we can have a walk on the sands. 4. (Spring, return), the flowers begin to bloom. 5. (The men, work hard), the wall was soon built. 6. (The sun, rise), we can now start. 7. (The boat, upset), the two boys had to swim ashore. 8. (He, absent), nothing can be done. 9. They think that the ship will be wrecked (a violent storm, rise). 10. (The audience, applaud), the musicians were much pleased. 11. (The town, capture), the inhabitants fled.

28. Verb and Complement.—We have shown that if the verb is Transitive, the Predicate consists of two main parts,—the Finite Verb and the Object.

Another subdivision of the Predicate is into Verb and **Complement.** There are some Transitive verbs, which, even after the Object has been expressed, do not make a complete sense until something more has been added for this purpose. The word or words thus added are called the Complement :—

They consider that house *too small for their wants.*
He made himself *quite at home in his friend's house.*

There are some Intransitive verbs, too, that require a Complement to make the sense complete :—

London has become *a very great city.*
The sun is *at a vast distance from the earth.*

I. Subject.	II. Predicate.		
	Finite Verb.	Object.	Complement.
London	has become	...	a very great city.
They	consider	that house	too small for their wants.
The sun	is	...	at a vast distance from the earth.
He	made	himself	quite at home in his friend's house.

Any kind of word or phrase, provided it makes sense and does not make bad grammar, may be used as a Complement.

Exercises on § 28. (To be done orally and at sight.)

(*a*) *Pick out the Object (if there is one) and the Complement in the following sentences* :—

1. The boy turned out very clever. 2. He is growing saucy. 3. I prefer London to Liverpool. 4. He set the prisoner free. 5. Delay is the thief of time. 6. Truth and honesty is the best policy. 7. He seems like a fish out of water. 8. We must cut the subject short. 9. I believe him to be perfectly honest. 10. This house is to let. 11. He is a good-natured man. 12. The results will soon be out. 13. The meeting appointed A. their chairman for that occasion. 14. He was called a fool, but the folly was on their side. 15. His health is getting worse and worse. 16. That pen is mine. 17. I felt very much hurt. 18. I am at your service. 19. All that glitters is not gold. 20. I am he. It is I.

(*b*) *Supply a Complement of some kind to the verb of each sentence*:—

1. The last Exhibition at Paris was ——. 2. He seems ——. 3. Our expectations did not come ——. 4. Henry V. of England was crowned ——. 5. A friend in need is ——. 6. The rain this year has been ——. 7. Cromwell was called ——. 8. Shakspeare is considered ——. 9. Paul of Tarsus was ——. 10. The girl does not seem ——. 11. The prisoner was declared ——. 12. Lord Roberts was appointed ——. 13. Gold is ——. 14. My health is growing ——. 15. The boy has become ——. 16. Vinegar tastes ——. 17. The country in which we live is called ——. 18. A man convinced against his will is ——. 19. The place of my birth was ——. 20. My age is ——. 21. My favourite study is ——. 22. My favourite game is ——. 23. The teacher has put the school ——. 24. Samuel anointed David ——. 25. The judge set the prisoner ——. 26. The jury declared him ——. 27. On calling at his house we found him ——. 28. The meeting elected him ——. 29. What is sauce for the goose is ——.

CHAPTER III.—FURTHER GRAMMATICAL RULES BEARING ON COMPOSITION.

SECTION 1.—RELATIVE AND INTERROGATIVE PRONOUNS.

29. Who, whom, which.—The forms *who* (Nominative) and *whom* (Objective) are used in reference to persons. The form *which* (both Nominative and Objective) is used in reference to things without life or to any kind of animal except man:—

The gardener *who* works here is ill. (*Nominative.*)
The gardener *whom* you employ is ill. (*Objective.*)

The wolf *which* seized the lamb has been shot. (*Nominative.*)
The wolf *which* you shot is dead. (*Objective.*)

30. "Who" or "which" as Subject of a verb.—A verb having *who* or *which* for its Subject or Nominative must be in the same number and the same person as the antecedent of *who* or *which* :—

(1) The boy who *has* come is hungry.
(2) The boy and girl who *have* come are hungry.
(3) I who *am* standing here wrote that letter.
(4) I am the man who *is* chosen for that work.

In (1) *who* is followed by *has*, a Singular verb in the Third person, because *boy*, the antecedent, is Singular and in the Third person.

In (2) *who* is followed by *have*, a Plural verb in the Third person, because the two antecedents *boy* and *girl* make a Plural, and both are in the Third person.

In (3) *who* is followed by *am*, a Singular verb in the First person, because *I*, the antecedent, is Singular and in the First person.

In (4) *who* is followed by *is*, a Singular verb in the Third person, because the antecedent *man* is Singular and in the Third person.

31. Whose, of which.—*Whose* is the Possessive form both of *who* and *which*. But when the antecedent denotes a thing or things without life, *of which* is rather more common than *whose*. The latter, however, has the merit of shortness and is often met with.

The tree under *whose* shade we were sitting.
The tree under the shade *of which* we were sitting.

32. Interrogative pronouns.—The forms of pronoun used for asking questions are shown below :—

Who spoke? (Nominative to the verb.)
Of *whom* did he speak? (Objective after Preposition.)

What did he say? }
Whom did he address? } (Objective after verb.)
Whose book is that? (Possessive.)
Which of these boys will win? (Selective form of Interrogative.)

Exercises on §§ 29-32. (To be done orally and at sight.)

(*a*) *Insert appropriate Relatives or Interrogatives in the places left blank* :—

1. The gentleman —— called this morning did not stop.
2. The wolf —— attacked the dog has been shot.
3. Where is the person about —— you were talking?
4. The fox, —— brush you are handling, was hunted a year ago.
5. I wish I could find the person —— he named.
6. The man —— you sent for arrived about an hour ago.
7. The box —— you packed so carefully was broken on the way.
8. The man —— lives here is a very steady workman.
9. The man and his wife —— live here seem very happy.
10. The wall —— was built two years ago is falling.
11. He wishes to punish me —— have done no wrong.
12. The sailor —— spoke to you will go to sea again soon.
13. The sailor —— you spoke to will go to sea again soon.
14. —— were you saying? —— did you speak to?
15. The man —— hat you are holding wants to put it on.
16. The cart in —— we rode is rather too rough.
17. The boy —— you were looking for has gone to school.
18. In —— school were your sons taught, and by ——?

19. Tell me —— of your sons will win the prize.

20. He —— fights and runs away will live to fight another day.

21. The house in —— we live was well built.

22. The garden —— stands near the house is well laid out.

23. The gardener —— has charge of it is called John.

24. In —— help do you trust most,—in mine or his?

25. The king —— reigns in this country is very popular.

26. The king for —— we fight deserves well of us all.

27. The farmer in —— field we are is coming towards us.

28. The farmer —— you addressed is an old friend of mine.

29. I —— am most concerned was not consulted.

30. I am the person —— is most concerned.

(*b*) *Correct any mistakes that you find in the following, and give the reason for the correction:—*

1. I am the person who go with you on that journey.

2. Here is the mason who you sent for to build the wall.

3. The prisoner whom I thought was guilty has been let off.

4. The girl and her brother who goes to that school fell ill on the way.

5. James, who you were looking for, has been found.

6. Whom do you think will be chairman at the next meeting?

7. Who did that box come from? Who was it addressed to?

8. Did any one tell you who they placed in charge?

9. I do not know who you are referring to.

10. The cleverest boy who we have in the school is absent to-day.

11. Whom do you suppose was the writer of that letter?

12. The goose who was lost yesterday has not been found.

13. I who tells you this can prove every word of it.

14. I am not the kind of person who am false.

15. You seem in a great hurry. Who are you expecting?

16. Who do you think I met this morning? My uncle.

17. Whom do you think spoke to me? Well: I must not say.

18. Who was that book sent by? I am sure I could not say.

19. The person whom you said was waiting is gone.

20. Who did you see there? Who were you talking to?

33. "That."—The word *that* is often used as a Relative for "who," "whom," or "which." When it is thus used, it never changes its form. It may therefore stand for a Nominative or an Objective; a Singular or a Plural; a Masculine, a Feminine, or a Neuter. But it can never be used for "whose" (Possessive).

Show me the house or houses *that* (=which) Jack built.
Show me the man or men *that* (=who) came.
Show me the man or men *that* (=whom) you wanted.

Whenever *that* is the Subject of a verb, take care that the verb is in the same number and the same person as the antecedent of *that*: see rule given in § 30.

This is the *man* that *does* it.
These are the *men* that *do* it.

Note.—After the adjective *same* the Relative *that* is more commonly used than *who, whom,* or *which,* and should therefore be used in preference:—

This is the same man *that* (=who) came before.
This is the same man *that* (=whom) we employed before.
This is the same box *that* (=which) we had before.

34. "As."—The word *as* is used as a Relative in the place of "who," "whom," or "which," when it comes after the adjective *such*. It may do the work of a Nominative or an Objective, but never of a Possessive.

He is not *such* a man *as* I wanted. (*Objective.*)
He is not *such* a man *as* you are. (*Nominative.*)

After the adjective *same*, the word *as* is used as a Relative, chiefly when there is no verb expressed after it:—

This book is the *same as* mine (is).

Whenever *as* is the Subject of a verb, take care that the verb is in the same number and the same person as the antecedent of *as*: see rule given in § 30.

Such *men* as they *were* are to be despised.
Such a *man* as he *was* is to be despised.

Exercise on §§ 33, 34. (To be done orally and at sight.)

Insert the proper Relative in the places left blank:—

1. The best thing —— you can do is to go to bed at once.
2. He is the cleverest student —— we have in the class.
3. To desert a man —— is a friend is a breach of friendship.
4. Such a wind —— that was destroyed almost every ship.
5. The same wind —— blew yesterday is blowing again to-day.
6. This is not the same book —— mine, but a rather larger one.
7. Such a voice —— yours will always be much admired.
8. He did not pass the same examination —— you did.

9. He did not pass the same examination —— you.

10. They made such a noise —— I never heard before.

11. Such trees —— grow in your garden are very beautiful.

12. This is my book —— I lent you two months ago.

13. The boy —— book you borrowed wishes to have it back.

14. I wish I could write you such a letter —— you wrote to me.

15. The letter —— you sent me gave me a great deal of pleasure.

16. The paper —— you wrote on is beautifully smooth and white.

17. Such a large house —— you live in would not suit my small income.

18. I am very fond of the garden —— is near the house.

19. The same kinds of flowers grow in my garden —— in yours.

20. The wallflowers —— grow near the porch are very pretty.

21. No flowers give such a scent —— roses do.

22. The scent —— roses give surpasses all other scents.

35. Precautions.—There are three errors to be guarded against:—

(*a*) The word *as* must not be used as a Relative, unless it is preceded by *such* or *same*:—

The man *as* I wanted has come. (Wrong. Say *whom* or *that*.)

(*b*) The word *such* is never followed by any kind of Relative except *as*. It is wrong, therefore, to say *such who, such whom, such which,* or *such that* in the place of *such as*:—

This is not *such* treatment *that* I expected. (Wrong. Say *such treatment as*.)

(*c*) The word *what* never has an antecedent. It

must therefore not be used in place of *who, whom, which,* or *that* :—

The boy *what* spoke must be punished. (Change to *who.*)

The box *what* came is full of books. (Change to *which* or *that.*)

I cannot remember *what* happened. (Correct.)

The last line is correct, because there is no antecedent to *what.*

Exercise on § 35. (To be done orally and at sight.)

Correct any mistakes that you find in the following :—

1. The grass as grows in this lawn is very coarse.
2. Such a man who came to-day is not fit for the work.
3. I return the book what you lent me three days ago.
4. I do not like any one as does not speak the truth.
5. The class what you teach is getting on well.
6. The carpenter as made that box is a very good workman.
7. I will tell you everything what I know about it.
8. Such things which they say are not to be believed.
9. The mason as built that wall built it crooked.
10. The matter what you inquire about does not concern you.
11. Such news that you brought spread quickly through the town.
12. Friendship is the virtue what I admire most.
13. He, not I, was the man as deceived you.
14. Most of all I like such scent that comes from roses.
15. The man what does not pay his debts is not honest.
16. A boy as is always talking can neither learn nor work.
17. The same book what you read last week I am reading now.

18. A bad potato is the worst thing as you will find anywhere.

19. This is the thing as he was meaning all the time.

20. Such things that do harm should be avoided.

SECTION 2.—ADJECTIVES AND ADVERBS: DEGREES OF COMPARISON.

36. How Adjectives and Adverbs differ.—Adjectives and Adverbs agree in one respect—both are *qualifying* words; that is, both modify the meaning of the word to which they belong.

What, then, is the difference? The difference is, that adjectives go with *nouns*, while adverbs go with *verbs*, *adjectives*, or other *adverbs*.

Another difference is in form.[1] Those adverbs that are formed from adjectives generally end in *ly*; as *beautiful* (adj.), *beautifully* (adv.).

She sings *beautiful*. (Wrong, change to *beautifully*.)
If it were so, it was a *grievous* fault,
And *grievously* hath Cæsar answer'd it.
SHAKSPEARE. (Right.)

Exercise on § 36. (To be done orally and at sight.)

Correct any mistakes that you may find in the following:—

1. He writes excellent: no one in the class can write as neat and clear as he does.
2. There is no fear: he will do it easy, even if you can't.
3. She walks very feeble after that long illness.
4. The man who said that will pay for it dear.
5. He reads rather indistinct, and requires practice.

---

[1] Some adverbs, however, have the same form as the corresponding adjectives, *i.e.* they do not end in *ly*; as *fast*, *hard*, *near*, *long*, *ill*, *much*, *little*, etc.

6. He will help you considerable, if you ask him.
7. They came to school very regular all last week.
8. He treated us all free and fair; so we can't complain.
9. The battle raged fierce from morning till evening.
10. That was noble spoken; it pleased me to hear it.
11. I am sure she did not upset the chair intentional.
12. They were all marvellous angry on hearing this.
13. He did it quite accidental; for he was more than half asleep.
14. I will act agreeable to your wishes in all things.
15. He spoke very intelligent; we all understood him.
16. He treated us handsome, and we ought to feel gratified.

Note 1.—Some adjectives end in *ly*; as "cowardly," "gentlemanly." We cannot make adverbs out of these by adding another *ly*. So instead of saying "cowardlily," we make an adverbial phrase, "in a cowardly way."

Note 2.—There are a few phrases in which the use of an adjective for an adverb is allowed by custom: "He speaks *loud* "The sun shines *bright*." This is a short way of saying "He is loud when he speaks"; "The sun is bright when it shines."

37. "Other" must be used after Positives and Comparatives.—When one thing is compared with another of the same kind or class, take care to use *other* after an adjective in the Positive or the Comparative degree:—

Positive.—He is as clever as any *other* boy in the class.
Comparative.—He is cleverer than any *other* boy in the class.

38. "Other" must not be used after Superlatives.—When one thing is said to surpass in a certain quality all other things of the same kind, take care not to use *other* after an adjective in the Superlative degree:—

The man, who of all *other* workmen was the laziest, professed to be the most industrious. (Wrong. Strike out the word *other*.)

39. Use of the Comparative degree.—When two things are compared with each other, it is more correct to use a Comparative than a Superlative :—

This boy is the *cleverest* of the two. (Change to *cleverer*.)

This boy is the *cleverest* of the three. (Correct.)

Exercises on §§ 37-39. (To be done orally and at sight.)

(*a*) *Correct any mistakes that you may find in the following* :—

1. England has more ships than any Power at the present time.
2. He is quite as serious in his sports as in any act of his life.
3. Sir M. P. was the most eminent of all other statesmen of his time.
4. The popularity of the Queen was greater than that of any monarch of her own time.
5. He did precisely what any man would do in the same circumstances.
6. That science, like every science, is based on certain first truths.
7. This one book secured more fame for its author than all his books put together.
8. The air of Nice is the most genial of any other spot in Europe.
9. London takes precedence of all English towns.
10. The state of the cotton-crop soon became known to the weavers of Manchester and to all concerned in the cotton trade.
11. Sir H. had the shortest memory of any other great statesman.

12. France prefers, with all the Powers, the policy of the open door in China.

13. Our troops have had some reverses, but no more than would have befallen any troops in a like situation.

14. Foreign aid is of no use for this or any purpose.

15. Gold is the most precious of all other metals.

16. Copper, though less precious, is more commonly used than any metal for purposes of coinage.

17. He understands the work better than any one of the same firm.

18. The tiger is the fiercest of the other wild beasts of the forest.

19. If I am to judge between James and John, the former seems to me the cleverest.

20. The cat is more domesticated than any animal of the tiger tribe.

21. If you compare a cat with a dog, the cat is the least faithful.

22. More rain has fallen in this than in any month of the year.

23. Which was the most celebrated city, Rome or Venice?

24. He writes quite as neatly as any boy in his class.

25. I have three sons, and J. is the more promising of the three.

26. Of the two countries, India and China, the last is the more populous.

27. Which is the best cricketer—Harry or James?

28. Poverty and vice—of these two enemies the last is by far the worst.

(*b*) *Reproduce the following sentences, substituting a Comparative for a Superlative, or a Superlative for a Comparative:—*

1. This student is cleverer than any other in the class.

2. A sharp ride on horseback is the best kind of exercise.

3. Of the three metals used for current coin, gold is heaviest.

4. Bombay is the safest seaport in India.
5. Bad health is the worst enemy that a man can have.
6. A. is the most industrious of my three sons.
7. The tiger is more fierce than any other wild beast.
8. Of all things in the world a voyage at sea is the healthiest.
9. Epic poetry stands higher than any other kind of poetry.
10. The best way to conquer a difficulty is to face it bravely.
11. England is the greatest naval power in the world.
12. China is more populous than any other country in the world.

(c) *Reproduce the following sentences, substituting a Positive for a Comparative, or a Comparative for a Positive, as shown below:—*

Positive. He is as dull as an ass.
Comparative. An ass is not duller than he is.

1. The air of hills is cooler than that of lowlands.
2. Bad health is a more terrible enemy than poverty.
3. This man has more debts than cash.
4. Certain other countries in the world are as hot as India.
5. Thou art much older in mind than in age.
6. It is easier to imagine this scene than to describe it.
7. A live ass is worth more than a dead lion.
8. Platinum is as heavy as gold.
9. A zebra is as swift-footed as an antelope.
10. He treats the poor with as much justice as he treats the rich.
11. You know his character as well as I do.
12. Exercise in the open air is more healthy than head-work.

Section 3.—Articles.

40. What Articles are.—Articles are really adjectives—*a* or *an* (the Indefinite article) being the shortest and simplest form of *one, any;* and *the* (the Definite article) the simplest form of *this, that, these, those.* Yet, for purposes of composition, the articles require a separate treatment.

41. A, an.—The form "*a*" is used before a consonant. It is also used before a vowel, when the vowel is sounded as if it were preceded by a consonant:—

A box. *A* chair. *A* useful thing. *A* ewe lamb. *A* one-eyed man.

We say *a useful*, not *an useful*, because *useful* is sounded as *yooseful.*

We say *a ewe*, not *an ewe*, because *ewe* is sounded as *yoo.* We say *a one-eyed*, not *an one-eyed*, because *one* is sounded as *wun.*

The form "*an*" is used before a vowel. It is also used before a consonant, when the consonant is not sounded:—

An ox. *An* omnibus. *An* hour. *An* heir. *An* honest man.

Exercise on § 41. (To be done orally and at sight.)

Correct, if necessary, the form of the Indefinite article in the following sentences:—

1. There is a inkspot on that paper. Ink is an useful article.
2. There was an heavy fall of snow in the night, and it filled an ewer standing in a open place.
3. King Rufus was shot by a arrow while riding an horse.
4. I never allow a organ to be played in front of my window.
5. A box of tools would be an useful present to him.
6. He gave a apple to one of them, and a orange to the other.
7. He drives an one-horse chaise at an uniform pace.

8. He is a untidy man, both in his work and his dress.
9. Have you an history of England to lend me?
10. He was a African by birth, not an European.
11. I want to buy a Arab horse.
12. He was kept two months laid up in an hospital.
13. We shall find a omnibus round the corner.
14. I never saw such a thing before; it was an unique sight.
15. There is a empty carriage in front, nearer the engine.
16. He was looked upon as an hero by all who knew him.
17. The snake that you saw was not an harmless one.
18. He is a unlikely person to do such a thing as that.
19. He was cheered with an universal shout of applause.
20. The motion was carried by an unanimous vote.
21. Have you a umbrella that you could lend me?

42. Repetition of Article.—If you wish to distinguish one person or thing from another, repeat the article (*a*) before the two nouns, or (*b*) before two adjectives qualifying the same noun. (See *Note* under § 2.)

(*a*) *Noun.* { *The* poet and *the* statesman *are* dead.
The poet and statesman *is* dead.

In the first sentence the repetition of the article shows that two distinct persons are intended, and therefore the verb (*are*) is plural. In the second sentence the non-repetition of the article shows that only one person is intended, and therefore the verb (*is*) is singular.

(*b*) *Adjective.* { I have *a* black and *a* white cat.
I have *a* black and white cat.

The first sentence means that I have *two* cats, one black and the other white. The second means that I have *one* cat, the colour of which is a mixture of black and white.

(*c*) Bring me *the* black and *the* white *cat.*
Bring me *the* black and white *cats.*
Bring me *the* black and white *cat.*

The last sentence refers to *one* cat, the colour of which is a mixture of black and white. The first and second sentences refer to *two* cats; to express this we can either repeat the Definite article and leave the noun Singular, or mention the article once and make the noun Plural.

43. Uses of "a."—To give a *general* sense to a noun we can use either (*a*) the Indefinite article before a Singular noun, or (*b*) no article at all before a Plural one:—

(*a*) *A man* cannot live long without food and drink.
(*b*) *Men* cannot live long without food and drink.

Sometimes "*a*" is used in the sense of "one" (its original meaning):—

A stitch in time saves *nine*.
A bird in the hand is worth *two* in the bush.

Sometimes no article is used even with a Singular noun:—

Man is a rational being. *Fire* burns.

44. Uses of "the."—To give a *particular* sense to a noun we use the Definite article (*the*), the noun being either Singular or Plural, according to the intention of the writer:—

The box has come. *The* boxes have come.

Here, of course, the writer is referring to some particular box or boxes, about which he knows something. Had he said "a box," this would imply that it was some box, about which he knew nothing.

Sometimes *the* is placed before a noun to denote a class or kind:—

The horse (*i.e.* the kind of animal which we call a horse) is a noble animal.

Here there is no real difference between "a horse," and "the horse."

Exercise on §§ 42-44. (To be done orally and at sight.)

Insert articles where they are needed, or remove superfluous ones; or change the number of the noun according to the requirements of the article:—

1. I have just bought a fresh copy of the Old and New Testament.

2. The five elements, according to the Hindoos, are the earth, the air, the fire, the water, and the ether.

3. Burnt child shuns the fire.

4. The old and new method of cure failed equally with him.

5. A cool and a bracing air suits me better than anything.

6. The black and the white horse that he rides fell with him.

7. I have to keep two servant-maids for this house, a cook and housemaid.

8. The just and the merciful general spared the conquered.

9. A live ass is better than dead lion.

10. Wise son maketh glad father; but foolish son is heaviness of his mother.—*Prov.* x. 1.

11. The men have a higher degree of reason than the brutes.

12. In building house use well-burnt bricks and a well-seasoned timber.

13. He was much respected both by the civil and military officers.

14. The men who have come are the pictures of health.

15. There is much difference between the English and Canadian climate.

16. I have had several voyages on the English, French, and German steamships, and I hardly know which I like best.

17. What steps can I take in face of your order?

18. The greatest traders in Europe are the English, Germans, and Dutch.

19. The loyal and disloyal members were agreed on this point.

20. Two horses were brought to me to choose from. I liked neither one nor the other.

21. No stranger a man than he ever entered this house.

22. The two parties, the Whig and Tory, were nearly equally balanced.

23. There are in this town a club, public library, and swimming-bath.

24. The secret societies in China could perhaps be distinguished under four heads—the tribal, industrial, the medical, and religious.

25. That state extends from the Hoang-ho to the British and French frontier.

26. The sale of a wife in the market-place is an habitual and an accepted fact among these savages.

27. Our party system is based on a manifest lie and crying wrong.

28. The wall which separated the Jews and Gentiles was broken down by the teaching of Christ.

29. This book is the work of a patient and an acute observer.

30. Between the higher and lower castes of India there is little or no difference of race.

31. It is not likely that the lion, tiger, or bear will ever become domesticated.

32. According to this writer, Richard I. showed himself at times in two opposite natures—the loved and loathed, spendthrift and a miser, king and a beggar, the bond and the free.

45. Omission of Article.—As a general rule, a Common noun in the Singular number should have some article placed before it. But the following exceptions should be noted.

(*a*) Names of titles and professions, when they precede a Proper noun :—

King Edward VII. Queen Victoria. Lord Ashley. Saint (St.) Paul. Judge Anson. General Roberts. Father Ignatius.

(*b*) Certain stock phrases consisting of a Transitive verb followed by its object :—

Strike root. Leave school. Give ear. Send word. Set foot. Shake hands. Keep house. Give battle. Cast anchor. Set sail. Take fire. Catch fire. Take breath. Follow suit. Do penance.

(*c*) Certain stock phrases consisting of a preposition followed by its object :—

By land. By water. On foot. On horseback. At sea. On board ship. At home. Under ground. In jail. Out of doors. By name. In fact. At school. In bed. By day. By night. Over head and ears. In debt. In trouble. At daybreak. At sunset. From head to foot. In court. At fault. At anchor. At ease. At sight. In sight. On demand. At dinner. At interest. In hand. On earth.

SECTION 4.—CHANGE OF FORM IN NOUN, PRONOUN, OR VERB.

46. Change of Number of noun.—If you are asked to rewrite a sentence in such a way as to change the number of the Subject from Singular to Plural, or from Plural to Singular, take care (1) to give the noun so changed its proper form as Singular or Plural; (2) to make the verb of the sentence agree in number with its Subject; (3) to make the pronoun of the sentence, if there is one, agree in number with its antecedent; (4) to change the number of any other word in the sentence, if this is required by the sense :—

Singular. The twig has begun to throw out a leaf from its bud.

Plural. The *twigs have* begun to throw out *leaves* from *their buds.*

Observe that the change of *twig* to *twigs* (*i.e.* the pluralising of the Subject) necessitates the change of *has* to *have*, *a leaf* to *leaves*, *bud* to *buds*, and *its* to *their*. The several words of the sentence are thus made to agree all round both in grammar and in sense.

Exercise on § 46. (To be done orally and at sight.)

Reproduce the following sentences, changing the number of the Subject or Subjects in each of them, and making any other changes required by grammar or by sense :—

1. A fly is a troublesome little thing when it settles on your face.
2. This shelf contains several books on difficult subjects.
3. The leaves have begun to lose their colours already.
4. The griefs which oppress me are hard to bear.
5. His foot is beginning to stumble, and the ankle aches.
6. The ox has hurt its hoof, and cannot draw the plough.
7. The sheep which is lying down has a heavy covering of wool.
8. The thief who was lately caught was almost a dwarf.
9. The man was armed with a knife, and the wolf fled.
10. He gave his life for his country, and was honoured as a hero.
11. The valley is green, and a deer is grazing in it.
12. The sow and the goose are in the same field together.
13. The poisonous gas had a bad effect, and the leaf withered.
14. A man must perform his duty, whether he likes it or not.
15. He is neither a thief nor a knave ; there is no proof.
16. The mouse has been playing to-day ; the cat is away.

17. The cow, followed by her calf, has been grazing all day.

18. A fish was seen in this pond; but I could not catch it.

19. The hoof of an ox is cloven; that of a horse is solid.

20. A negro deserves to be free as much as a white man.

21. The key of the box was lost; so the lock had to be picked.

22. The grotto in the garden is almost buried under evergreens.

23. The motto that he quoted is well worthy of attention.

24. The loaf was divided, and every one had his share.

25. This man is quite a genius, anything but a goose.

26. A dormouse is a great sleeper; let it sleep on.

27. The valley resounds, and the echo is heard far and wide.

28. The roof of that house leaks; it needs repairing.

47. Nouns in the Possessive case.—A Singular Possessive is formed by adding *apostrophe s;* a Plural by adding only the apostrophe.

Singular. A *horse's* tail. | *Plural.* *Horses'* tails.

If the Plural does not end in *s*, the Possessive Plural is formed in the same way as the Possessive Singular.

Singular. A *man's* hat. | *Plural.* *Men's* hats.

Exercise on § 47. (Can be best done in writing.[1])

Reproduce the following sentences, changing the number of the Possessive, and making any other changes that may be necessitated either by grammar or by sense:—

[1] In consequence of the importance of putting the apostrophe in the right place, it would be advisable that most of these examples should be written out.

1. My niece's book has been left on the shelf: she is careless.
2. The thief's trick was found out through his own carelessness.
3. The horse's hoof will be hurt if it is not shod.
4. Did you see any lady's cloak in this room?
5. A mistress's order must be obeyed by her pupils.
6. Many an ox's hide was brought into the market and sold.
7. Try to rescue that ship's crew before the ship is lost.
8. Put broken glass in a mouse's hole, and the mouse will go away.
9. He was much amused at the sight of the monkey's tail.
10. A fox's tail is much valued: this is why the fox is hunted.
11. We have found the robbers' cave; they will soon be caught.
12. A man's muscles are stronger than a woman's.
13. A signal-man's box must be put up in its proper place.
14. A man's hat is not always an ornament to his head.
15. A bird's beak is sometimes curved and sometimes straight.
16. The camel's back is sore: it had too much to carry, and the saddle did not fit.
17. A librarian's salary is seldom as high as it should be.
18. Was the lady's umbrella ever found?
19. The witnesses' evidence was not to be believed.
20. The songstresses' notes gave us much pleasure.
21. The lioness's roar was heard far and wide.
22. The ladies' umbrellas can be placed in this corner.
23. The workmen's pay is not as high as it should be.
24. We have heard the witness's statement on the opposite side.
25. The teacher's word must be at once obeyed.

26. The seamstress's work was excellent.
27. The duchess's jewel has been found by the police.
28. The actresses' costumes were very peculiar.
29. A hero's exploits will always be remembered.
30. The wolf's long-drawn howl was heard in the distance.
31. The dwarf's arm was as short as that of a child.
32. It gladdens us to hear the cuckoo's note.
33. Much attention was paid to the negro's complaint.
34. The wife's quarters were well planned and well built.
35. I dislike to hear the goose's cackling.
36. The lass's hat can be hung up on this peg.
37. The tigresses' whelps were shot, but not the lioness's.
38. The monkey's tricks made every one laugh.
39. The puppy's playfulness was equal to the kittens'.
40. The donkey could not keep up with the horse's pace.
41. The horses despised the donkeys' pace, and went far ahead.

48. Possessive pronouns.—Personal pronouns have two different forms of Possessive:—

First form. My, thy, her, our, your, their.
Second form. Mine, thine, hers, ours, yours, theirs.

The first is used when it stands before the noun with which it is connected in sense:—

My book. Her book. Our books. Your books. Their books.

The second is used (*a*) when it is separated from the noun by a verb coming between; (*b*) when no noun is expressed after it; (*c*) when it is preceded by *of*:—

(*a*) This book is *mine*. That house is *theirs*.
(*b*) My horse and *yours* (your horse) are both tired.
(*c*) That horse of *yours* is tired.

Precaution:—

There is no second form for *his*: the form *hisn*, which is heard among certain classes, is not English. We must not say *ourn* for *ours*, *hern* for *hers*, *yourn* for *yours*, or *theirn* for *theirs*. These are heard only in low life. The only Possessives that end in *n* are *mine*, *thine*.

Let it be observed also that *ours*, *hers*, *yours*, *theirs*, although the final *s* is the Possessive sign, have no apostrophe written between the *r* and the *s*, as in *father's* and all other nouns in the Singular number.

Exercise on § 48. (To be done orally and at sight.)

Insert the right form of Possessive pronoun in the places where a Personal pronoun is enclosed in brackets. Correct also any errors which you may find:—

1. That manner of (you) is not as good as it should be.
2. The book which you are reading is (I), not (he).
3. (I) horse is not so strong as (you) or (he).
4. (He) cow gives much more milk that mine or yourn.
5. What he calls (he) property is not really (he).
6. The poet prefers (he) own poem to (you) or (she).
7. That house of (they) is very handsomely furnished.
8. (I) house and (you) were built on precisely the same plan.
9. (She) wishes are of no importance compared with yourn.
10. That face of (she) looks more wrinkled than (I).
11. I wish I had seen that letter of (you) before I posted (I).
12. That box is hisn, not yourn; so leave it where it was.
13. The hat which you wear is larger than mine or hisn.
14. Mary has chosen the better part, and that part shall be hern.

15. The parcel in your hand is theirn, so let them have it.

16. My height is not the same as yourn; you are the taller.

17. That shilling is not mine, but hisn; my father gave it me.

49. Reflexive or Emphatic pronouns.—The Reflexive forms of Personal pronouns are used for two purposes—(*a*) to show that the person (or thing) does something to himself (or itself); (*b*) to make a Personal pronoun more emphatic.

(*a*) I hid *myself*.	(*b*) I *myself* did it.

Precautions:—

(1) In the first and second persons the Possessive form of the Simple pronoun is used before "self"; as *myself*, *ourselves*; *yourself*, *yourselves*. But in the third person we use the objective before "self"; as *himself*, *herself*, *itself*, *themselves*. It is wrong therefore to say *his self*, *their selves*.

(2) It is not correct to use the Reflexive or Emphatic form as the Subject of a sentence, unless it is accompanied by some noun or by the simple form of the corresponding pronoun, as:—

Myself saw it. (Change to *I myself*.)

Exercise on § 49. (To be done orally and at sight.)

Correct any mistakes that you may find in the following:—

1. He hurt his self badly in falling over that rock.
2. You must have seen him; myself saw him distinctly.
3. Bees provide their selves with honey against the winter.
4. He sold his umbrella, and has bought his self a new one.

5. The girl is seated in the field: herself brought the chair.

6. They, and not himself, paid the penalty of his faults.

7. Both herself and Mary were wandering in the wood.

8. John his self will pay for the book that he lost.

9. Why do they injure their selves in that way?

10. "Is he hooked, do you think?" whispered Crimple, as himself and partner stood watching him in a distant part of the room.—DICKENS.

11. War, as himself avowed, was necessary to his hold on France.

12. They dressed their selves out in all their best clothes.

13. Jane was waiting for them: himself saw them go in.

14. He did his self no good by losing his temper.

15. He never acted thus when himself was in office.

16. That is his book: he paid for it his self.

50. The Future tense.—The Future tense, Indicative, is formed with **shall** in the *First* person, and with **will** in the *Second* and *Third* persons:—

	1	2	3
Singular.	I *shall* go.	Thou *wilt* go.	He *will* go.
Plural.	We *shall* go.	You *will* go.	They *will* go.

If *will* is used in the First person, it expresses not merely Future time, but intention. Thus "I *will* go" means "I *intend* to go." "It is *my will* to go." "I am *willing* to go."

If *shall* is used in the Second or Third person, it expresses not merely Future time, but an order, or a promise, or a threat, or a confident assurance. Thus "he *shall* go" means that, in compliance with some order, promise, threat, or confident prediction, he will have to go.

Note.—The word *not* or any other adverb is placed between the Auxiliary verb and the Principal one; as "He will *not* go," "He will *certainly* go."

Exercises on § 50. (To be done orally and at sight.)

(*a*) *Insert the proper form of Future in the places where the verb is indicated in brackets. Nothing but Future time is to be expressed in the following sentences:—*

1. I hope he (be) in time to catch the first train.
2. I believe that we (see) the procession after all.
3. The time (come), when you (see) the force of my words.
4. He not (fail) to fulfil his promise; there is no fear.
5. We (be) very glad to see him, if only he (come).
6. Our country (fight) to the bitter end; we (fear) nothing.
7. I expect we (have) a better man for leader than you (have).
8. As soon as he hears the result, he (send) us a report of it.
9. A disappointed man always (raise) the cry of "Sour grapes."
10. I don't know how we (get) our money back.
11. I cannot now give as much time as I (be forced) to give next week.
12. Of course he (give) security for the loan; you (lose) nothing.

(*b*) *Reproduce the following sentences, so as to bring out the full force of "shall" or "will" wherever the context shows that these words are used in a sense that denotes something more than Future time:—*

1. The time will come, when you shall hear me.
2. I will not consent to that, whatever you may say.
3. "Rome shall perish," said the Druid; "her fate is sealed."

4. The fear of the Lord shall cover the whole earth.

5. If you take a man's life, you shall be hanged.

6. Thou shalt not steal. Thou shalt not bear false witness.

7. He shall receive his prize to-morrow, and I hope that he will be satisfied with it.

8. Charles, I thank thee for thy love to me, which thou shalt find I will most kindly requite.

9. "I will be drowned; nobody shall save me," said a man who was bent on destroying his own life.

10. The parcel shall be delivered at your door by the evening.

11. I will never do such a thing again; no, never.

12. If you come too late to-morrow, you shall be fined.

13. We will spend almost any amount to secure this site.

14. You shall not admit strangers into any of our rights.

15. We will not vote any money to help the cause of our enemies.

16. They shall pay dearly for it, if they treat us so again.

17. An idler and a wine-bibber shall not go unpunished.

(*c*) *Correct any misuse of "shall" or "will" that you may find in the following sentences:*—

1. It may be hoped that such misconduct shall not occur again.

2. A few years hence we will find him very much improved.

3. It shall go hard with our generals, if they are misjudged by their fellow-countrymen.

4. We expect that the Government shall do what is necessary.

5. If the rain falls in time, we and our country shall not suffer.

6. I cannot think what the Jews shall say about the great Jew of Tarsus.

7. Who can tell what shall be the greatest event in the new century?

8. We shall not be surprised, if the Queen's visit to Ireland shall mark the beginning of the reunion of hearts.

9. We are about to publish a history which we hope shall satisfy the public.

10. These little faults will not displease any one who shall turn to this book for solace and instruction.

11. I feel assured that I will not be misunderstood.

12. Considering that two thousand Puritan preachers resigned on the Restoration, who shall say that the Puritans were not genuine men?

13. The money has been stolen, but the owner thinks that he shall get it back in a day or two.

14. Not until this is done, will we have any guarantee that we shall not be ruined.

15. Great dangers are before us, unless it shall be found possible to demand a remedy.

16. This has happened before, and no doubt we will see it happen again.

17. So long as the army is mismanaged, we will never be prepared when the time of danger comes.

51. Present and Past tenses.—In Strong verbs (miscalled Irregular) the Past tense is *not* formed by adding *t* or *d* to the Present, but only by *some change of inside vowel.* In Weak verbs the Past tense is formed by adding *t* or *d* to the Present, and (with a few exceptions) there is no change of the inside vowel. Care must be taken to form the Past tense correctly.[1]

Exercise on § 51. (To be done orally and at sight.)

Rewrite the following sentences, changing the verbs from the Present tense to the Past, or vice versâ:—

---

[1] *To the Teacher.*—The Exercises under §§ 50, 51, 52 all presuppose that the students have been well-grounded in the accidence of English Grammar. In fact, as was stated at the outset, the exercises in grammar contained in this book are not intended to supersede the study of grammar, but to supplement it. Students who have been well versed in accidence can easily read off these exercises at sight.

1. The dentist draws out a tooth for me this morning.
2. The mouse creeps from its hole when no one is near.
3. I beseech him to be careful what he says.
4. The plank bends as you stand upon it.
5. The finger bleeds a good deal where it is cut.
6. The sun rises at six o'clock and sets about the same time.
7. He abides with me for the night and leaves in the morning.
8. He lies awake for two hours and then sleeps again for two more.
9. She bears her sorrow bravely, as becomes her resolute character.
10. A storm sweeps across the scene and brings disaster.
11. The birds build their nests and feed their young.
12. They bid him farewell, and some begin to weep.
13. He bought a book and kept it carefully.
14. Familiarity breeds contempt, as he plainly shows.
15. They bind him hand and foot, and hold him fast.
16. The hare speeds along the field, but the dog catches it.
17. The dog bites the wolf, and clings to it with its teeth.
18. When a small boy beats a bully, no one weeps at the sight.
19. One seeks for the metal, the other gilds it.
20. The wind blows cold; but yet spring comes back to us in its season.
21. A fire burns up all his property and he sells nothing.
22. He girds on his sword and meets his enemy for combat.
23. The gardener digs deep and breaks up the clods.
24. The just man deals fairly with all, and tells them what to expect.
25. She teaches the boy to understand what he reads.
26. They chide the soldier, who fights badly.
27. He who chooses the best way of working finds his reward.
28. No one dreams of keeping what another lends him.

29. He drinks to his friend's health and flings down the cup.

30. This man drives the engine which grinds the wheat.

31. They lead the stranger to the home where his friend dwells.

32. He eats a good breakfast and rings the bell for his horse.

33. The fox runs as hard as he can and falls into the trap.

34. I feel much sorrow, when a man shoots a dove.

35. The skylark flies up to a great height, when the sun shines.

36. He forbears to tell me what that machine costs.

37. We all forget the song that she sings best.

38. The bird never forsakes its nest, but sits there till the young are hatched.

39. The child kneels on the floor and leans against the bed.

40. The air grows colder and colder, and the water freezes in the pipes.

41. He gets very tired, when he swims for nine minutes.

42. He gives way to his betters and stands somewhere else.

43. The cat smells a mouse and sits near the hole watching.

44. The thief hides for an hour or two and then slinks away.

45. I know the word which he spells so wrongly.

46. The high priest rends his garment when he hears that.

47. The cat lies under the bush and springs upon the rabbit.

48. He slings the bag over his shoulder and goes away.

49. He means what he says and sends the man away.

50. He never thinks twice, and sticks to what he intends.

51. A horseman rides past, and sees what they are doing.

52. The sun rises at six o'clock, and lights up the eastern horizon.

53. He spends all his spare time at work, and does all he can to pay his way.

54. The earthquake shakes the ground; men's hearts sink with fear.

55. The spider spins its web and strives to catch a fly.

56. David slays the giant and smites him with the sword.

57. I shrink from that task; I dare not undertake it.

58. The boy slides on the ice; a fall seldom hurts him.

59. While he speaks, the thief steals his purse.

60. He takes the first opportunity and strikes while the iron is hot.

61. He strides along in his pride and swings his walking stick.

62. A man who swears falsely throws aside all self-respect.

63. She spills her tea through carelessness and spoils her dress.

64. He tears up the letter and throws it into the fire.

65. He treads the same road as usual and wears the same dress.

66. While the daughter weaves, the mother writes a letter.

67. The wasp stings the man, who seizes the honey.

68. He who conquers himself wins a great victory.

69. She strings the beads and winds them round her neck.

70. On hearing such news she wrings her hands with grief.

71. The wood-cutter cleaves the stump in two with his axe.

52. Past tenses and Past participles.—In Strong verbs the Past tense often differs in form from the Past participle. Care must therefore be taken not to use the one where we ought to use the other.

Care must also be taken not to give a Strong verb the Weak form of Past tense or Past participle:—

(1) I will leave the house, but I will not be *drove* out.
(2) I *seed* him coming all the time.

In (1) *drove* (Past tense) must be changed to *driven* (Past participle). In (2) *seed* (Weak past) must be changed to *saw* (Strong past).

Exercise on § 52. (To be done orally and at sight.)

Correct any errors that you find in the following, and give the correct conjugation (Present tense, Past tense, and Past participle) of each verb :—

1. Let us get up : the sun has rose ; it is now daylight.
2. I wish to know who done that : he shall be drove out for it.
3. His sufferings were all bore with great patience.
4. His cheek was bit by a gnat, and is very much swelled.
5. I have began to learn Latin : you begun two years ago.
6. The straw was blowed about the house in all directions.
7. Everything has gone wrong; I am completely broke.
8. He has chose the very best fruit in the garden.
9. He gone home three weeks ago for a holiday.
10. They sung a song and drunk each other's health.
11. He had forgot that he had ate his dinner, and asked for more.
12. They were almost drove to despair by the failure of that bank.
13. The horse had fell down and broke its knees.
14. The birds flied away when the ground was froze, and they could find nothing to eat.
15. He was forsook by his friends ; they gived him no help.
16. He growed so much in one year, that no one knowed him again.
17. He had rode forty miles, and was much shook with the labour.
18. They shrunk back, when he sunk at last in the water.
19. They slayed the mad dog, which had bit the girl.

20. The thieves that have stole the watch will be caught.

21. A word, when it has once been spoke, cannot be recalled.

22. He was smit with her beauty and has wrote to her.

23. They have strove to do better, and have took much pains.

24. The letter was tore to pieces and throwed on the floor.

25. That dress is nearly wore out; it was wove by hand.

26. He awaked at five o'clock and begun to dress.

27. He digged for two hours before food was took to him.

28. Who rung that bell? and who run down to answer it?

29. The sun shined very bright on the day when we come back.

30. She sung two songs before she sat down.

31. The rabbit sprung into the water and swum across.

32. She sung a song, as she winded the thread round a reel.

33. This school was beat by that at football.

34. The plank was cloved asunder at one blow of the axe.

35. The camel was heavily laded before they started.

36. By four o'clock the lawn was well mowed.

37. The log, that was sawed in two, was quite rotted.

38. He was showed how to do it, and so he did it well.

39. Has he sowed the seed? The ground is strewed with dead leaves.

40. The horse had drank too much, so it run slowly.

41. The driver has mistook the road: he took the wrong turn.

42. He see me as I was bringing the letter that I had wrote.

43. The canal is now froze over, and the price of coal has rose.

44. My mother teached me to write, and my father to spell.

53. Verbs apt to be confounded.—Take care not to confound the following verbs:—*lie, lay* (place): *rise, raise* (lift): *fall, fell* (cut down or knock down): *sit, set* (place). In each pair the first is Intransitive, the second Transitive.

Exercise on § 53. (To be done orally and at sight.)

Correct the mistakes, if you find any, in the following, and give the correct conjugation (Present tense, Past tense, and Past participle) of each verb :—

1. The man laid down for a few minutes to take some rest.
2. The hen has lain a egg on the straw of the stable.
3. He rose it up as high as he could above his shoulders.
4. The tree felled heavily down with a sudden crash.
5. The leopard has not yet learnt to lay down with the kid.
6. We can set down here a little, till we have rested.
7. The dead bodies were laying scattered about on the battlefield.
8. The hens have begun to set: we shall get some chickens.
9. Lay the books in their proper order on the shelves.
10. The matter was laid before the proper authority.

Section 5.—Sequence of Tenses.

54. Two main rules.—There are two main rules regarding the sequence of tenses:—

Rule I.—A Past tense in the Principal clause must be followed by a Past tense in the Dependent clause:—

Principal clause.	*Dependent clause.*
It *was* settled,	that I *should* do this.
He *would* come,	if you *wished* it.
He *was* honest,	although he *was* poor.
He *asked* me,	whether I *had* seen his dog.
He *was* informed,	that I *had* been helping him.

Principal clause.	*Dependent clause.*
We never *understood*,	how or why he *did* that.
He *did* not leave off,	till he *had* succeeded.
I *was* inquiring,	what you *had* heard.
He *gained* his end,	because he *worked* hard.
He remained silent,	as soon as he *heard* that.
I *would* do this,	if *I were* allowed.
He *walked* so far,	that he *tired* himself.

Exceptions :—

(1) If the verb in the Dependent clause expresses some *universal* or *habitual* fact, it is in the Present tense :—

He *was* taught, that the earth *moves* round the sun.
We *were* informed, that his character *is* good.

(2) After "than" the verb can be in any tense that expresses the sense intended by the speaker or writer :—

He *liked* you better than he *likes* or *liked* or *will like* me.

Rule II.—A Present or a Future tense in the Principal clause can be followed in the Dependent clause by any tense that is required by the sense :—

I *know* that he *was*, *is*, or *will be* angry.
I *shall* soon hear what he *says*, *said*, or *will say*.

Exercises on § 54. (To be done orally and at sight.)

(*a*) *Supply the tense and voice of the verb enclosed in brackets* :—

1. I hoped that you (will) return soon after the sun (go) down.
2. I hope that you will be more industrious than you (be) last term.
3. He trusted that peace (will) soon be made.
4. He tried how many miles he (can) walk in an hour.
5. He did not go away, till the work of the term (be) over.

6. The oxen lowed so loud that we (find) out where they (be).

7. I went to his house, that I (may) tell him all that (happen).

8. It was not likely that he (will) catch the train.

9. He has been so disappointed that he (will) not try again.

10. There was a rumour that he (perish) in the fire, which (break) out in the village yesterday.

11. I signed my name on the understanding that you (will) keep your engagement with me.

12. Your son did better than I (expect) he (will).

13. His voice trembled so much that I (feel) suspicious.

14. I gave him no answer for fear that I (may) annoy him.

15. He came upon me as suddenly as if he (have) dropped from the sky.

16. He made up his mind that such a thing (shall) not happen again.

17. It made no difference to him how we (carry) on the business.

18. We would not take him into partnership, if he (ask) us.

19. He told me that he (be) about to visit his native village.

20. They guarded the door so that he (may) not escape.

21. He had friends outside, who (will) bring him secret help, if the guards (be) not careful.

22. There have been many signs, that his cause (will) triumph.

23. We were willing to take him, provided he (be) willing to come.

24. The admiral declared that a world-trade without a proper fleet (remind) him of a cavalry man who (can) ride well, but (have) no horse.

25. A man of whom I asked the question denied that this (be) so.

26. He announced that he (feel) confident that the

trouble (will) soon be over, if all persons concerned (will) work well together.

27. The committee recommended that if Mr. S. (will) cover the shed with a solid roof, he (shall) be granted a licence for five years.

28. The expedition was, so far as its object (is) concerned, a failure.

29. They unintentionally disclosed their belief that the struggle (be) hopeless.

30. He issued an order that no one (shall) be molested on account of the opinions that he (express).

31. It would be a disgrace to the Government, if nothing (be) done to redress this wrong.

32. He could not have done so well, unless an opportunity, which he (dare) not throw away, (present) itself.

33. It was unfortunately the case that the Japanese, who (have) settled down in Corea, (belong) to a very low class.

34. He expressed the fear that the designs of France (will) be accomplished, before England's voice (be) raised.

35. No man has ridden to hounds more often than the late Mr. Bevan (do).

36. The result of the operations was that the two generals (occupy) secure positions.

(b) *Correct any mistakes that you may find in the following; the Principal verb must not be changed:—*

1. He telegraphed last night that he has occupied a strong position.

2. It is unlikely that any difficulty would be caused.

3. I was led into it by what are obviously false pretences.

4. Our interests demand that there should not be two rival sects.

5. He stated yesterday that he has received no further news.

6. A reward has been offered to the first man who succeeded in rehoisting the flag over Pretoria.

7. It will be well, if one or two of those who are responsible were hanged.

8. The engineers have declared that the last section of the railway would be completed by the promised date.

9. They have patted the rustic on the back and told him what a fine fellow he was.

10. The filching of that port stirred up the rivalries of the Powers at a time when they bid fair to sleep a long sleep.

11. It is highly desirable that an enemy should see another wall of defence behind the first, and a third behind the second, so that the whole prospect might be too alarming to tempt an invader.

12. The hope was expressed that the Board of Education will introduce some changes in the curriculum of Training Colleges.

13. What we hope is this, that the work we do may be consecrated to God, and that He might accept and bless it.

14. It might be expected that generous treatment will obtain their willing co-operation and consent.

15. It was not deemed likely in official circles that the German reply will be published.

16. The clause provides that such questions only should be referred to the Supreme Court of Appeal.

17. Sir W. took his stand on the principle that the first elements of living matter consisted of cells.

18. Were he still disposed to go there, my purse shall be open to him.

19. Public affairs would become one network of confusion, if these men shall succeed in getting the upper hand.

20. I was never so long in company with a girl, trying to entertain her, and succeed so ill.

21. Though much of our care may prove to be useless, the satisfaction would remain of having done all that prudence suggests.

22. Pilate challenged the Jews to prove that public opinion is on their side and against Jesus.

23. He stated that men like himself, who were behind the scenes, knew that the progress, though slow, is steady.

24. Sir Roger was saying last night that none but men of fine parts deserve to be hung.—STEELE, *Spectator*, No. 6.

25. It has always been said by experts that there was in the Colonies the finest military material in the world.

CHAPTER IV.—COMBINATION OF SIMPLE SENTENCES.

SECTION 1.—TO COMBINE SIMPLE SENTENCES INTO A SIMPLE SENTENCE.

55. Modes of combination.—The principal modes, in which two or more Simple sentences can be combined so as to make one Simple sentence, are shown in the following examples. Observe that in the combined sentence there is never more than *one* Finite verb,.and hence every sentence so combined is Simple (that is, *single*).

(*a*) *By using Participles which shall qualify the Subject or the Object:*—

Separate. He took his hat from the peg. He left the house.

Combined. Taking, or having taken, his hat from the peg he left the house.

(*b*) *By using Participles in the absolute construction:*—

Separate. The sun rose. The fog dispersed.

Combined. The sun having risen, the fog dispersed.

(*c*) *By using Prepositions with nouns or gerunds:*—

Separate. The sun went down. The work was not yet completed.

Combined. { The sun went down before the completion of the work.
The work was not completed by sunset.

(*d*) *By using Infinitives for Finite verbs* :—

Separate. He has four sons. They must all be started in life.

Combined. He has four sons to start in life.

(*e*) *By using nouns or phrases in apposition* :—

Separate. The faithful dog lay by the cradle. Its name was Bethgelert.

Combined. The faithful dog, Bethgelert by name, lay by the cradle.

Exercises on § 55. (To be done orally and at sight.[1])

(*a*) *Combine the following sentences after the manner shown in* (*a*). *The main verb is indicated by italics* :—

1. He wrote down all the answers. He still *had* time to revise them.
2. He held his walking-stick under his arm. He *walked* up and down the street.
3. He arrived in town in the forenoon. He *went* at once to the best shop.
4. The dogs are placed in different kennels. So they *cannot* quarrel.
5. They were not able to convict him by direct proof. So they *injured* his character by slander.
6. The travellers hung up their hats. They *sat* down to rest.
7. Her father was a very successful tradesman. He *was* able to leave her a great deal of money.
8. He bought a good house. He furnished it well. He *brought* his family to live in it.

---

[1] *To the Teacher.*—We offer two recommendations as to the method of working out the examples in this chapter: (1) let the student be told to read out the example *slowly* to the class before he begins to make the attempt to combine the sentences contained in it ; (2) to prevent a student from looking ahead and preparing for the example which will fall to his turn, let the examples be taken in any order announced by the teacher, and not in the serial order of the figures. After a little practice the examples in Sections 1 and 2 can be easily worked out at sight by any student of average intelligence.

9. He tripped all of a sudden. He *let* the basket with all its contents fall off his head.

10. I disliked the noise of London streets. I *returned* to my quiet house in the country.

11. The prince arrived with his courtiers. He was *received* by the citizens with a great deal of cheering.

12. Sir Ralph the Rover enriched himself with plunder. He *was turning* his ship towards a secret port.

13. The prince stood silently in the crowd. No one *recognised* him.

14. The general *told* his men to seize a hill. That hill is now known as the Western Heights.

15. He was much pleased with the cleverness of the answer. He *forgave* the rudeness.

16. He was inspired with hope. He climbed up the precipice. He *reached* the top in safety.

17. The measurements were carried out by the best engineer in the force. Such measurements *could* hardly fail to be correct.

18. He raised his hand towards the audience. He thus *commanded* silence.

19. The sea *threatened* to overwhelm the boat. The boat was tossed by the waves.

20. He had fought bravely for his country. He *was honoured* with a public funeral after his death.

21. King Bruce of Scotland saw the perseverance of the spider. Its perseverance was crowned with success. He therefore *made up* his mind to make one more attempt.

22. The sportsman took up his gun. The gun was lying in a corner of the hall. He *went out* after a tiger.

23. The wild boar *charged* the rider. The rider was then turning round to attack it with his spear.

24. The horse got loose from its stable. It ran out into the open field. It *snorted* with excitement.

25. The boatmen *looked out* eagerly for land. They had lost their way in the fog. The fog surrounded them on all sides.

26. They *perceived* a faint light in the distance. The light came from a village bonfire.

27. He at last *found* his sister. She was seated in a grotto. She was reading a book.

28. The beadle rang the bells. He awakened the villagers with the ringing. He then *led* them away to the burning house.

29. The prisoner *saw* a flower from the window of his cell. The flower smiled upon him in his sorrow.

30. The wood-pigeon saw her mate shot dead before her. She *was terrified* at the suddenness of the blow.

31. I saw a flickering light in the distance. It appeared to come from a ship out at sea. I *stood* watching it for nearly an hour.

32. The horse *picked* itself up in a moment. It had stumbled in the dark against a large stone.

33. Wolves *were heard* in the distance. They were howling for prey.

34. His mode of welcome appeared to be insincere. It *gave* me no pleasure. It gave me no comfort.

35. Cowper's dog was called Beau. It plunged into the river Ouse. It *swam out* to secure the lily. The lily was the one desired by the poet, its master.

36. Some French soldiers at Boulogne seized the young English sailor. They led him away to Napoleon's tent. On the way they *ridiculed* his little boat. It was built by him for crossing over to England.

37. Instead of mirth and festivity we *saw* nothing but sorrow. It saddened every face. It darkened the bright lights of the banquet hall.

38. The ploughman was returning home in the evening. He suddenly *turned back*. He heard his child's voice. The child was singing merrily behind a hedge.

39. In the midst of the forest we heard the voice of the cuckoo. But we were unable to see the bird. We *returned* home. We were much disappointed.

(*b*) *Combine the following sentences after the manner shown in* (*b*). *The main verb is indicated by italics:—*

1. The spring is now well advanced. We *shall* soon *hear* the cuckoo's voice again.

2. The dog plunged into the river. The fish scudded away in terror. We *had* bad sport for the next half-hour.

3. The horses were taken out of the traces. The carriage *was drawn* along by the eager crowd.

4. The war was over. The country was pacified. The volunteers *were sent* back to their homes.

5. His eldest son was fond of travel. The head of the firm *handed over* the management of his business to his second son.

6. He remained behind. The *rest* set off at 2 o'clock P.M.

7. The town was relieved at last. The British forces entered. The enemy *retreated* in confusion.

8. The admiral brought all his ships into port. The crews *had* a little recreation on shore.

9. The facts are decidedly in favour of your innocence. You *are acquitted* of the charge.

10. The house was enclosed by a garden. The garden was enclosed by a high wall. The garden-thieves *could* not carry off any of the fruit.

11. The berry is now ripe. It is fit to be plucked. We *shall have* plenty of seed for next year's crop.

12. This pupil has been idle the whole of the past term. There is no hope of his making up for lost time. The headmaster advised his parents to remove him from the school.

13. He called for his gun. He took a good aim. The mad dog *was shot.*

14. He refused to open his door. The unwelcome visitors *went away.*

15. The defendant was too ill to bear the fatigue and anxiety of a lawsuit. The case *was postponed* for two weeks.

16. The men had no ammunition left. They were being surrounded by the enemy. The general *ordered* a retreat.

17. We made our bow to the Prince. We politely retired. The next man *came* forward with his petition.

18. The demand for labour was very slack. The poor men *could* earn very little.

19. The pitmen were divided into two factions. They could not agree. The work *was carried* on with much difficulty and delay.

20. Every farmer has been provided with a yoke of oxen. The fields *will* soon *be ploughed* up for the next harvest.

21. They have reached a place of safety. No further danger *need* now be expected.

22. Some straw was laid on the ground. The blankets were spread on the straw. The soldiers, after their long march, *had* a good sleep.

23. The judge entered the court. He took his seat at the bench. The trial *proceeded*.

24. The tree on the edge of the river was cut down by the woodman. It fell into the water. The crash and splash *could* be heard a great distance off.

25. He lost his purse. A great search was made. Some one *discovered* the purse at last in the lining of his coat.

26. They gave him ample food for refreshment. He *was* able to pursue his journey with greater energy.

27. A brief halt was made for luncheon. The army then *resumed* its march.

28. Columbus related the story of his wonderful voyage. The king and queen of Spain *fell* on their knees in thankfulness to God.

29. The king and queen fell on their knees. All present *followed* their example.

30. The hounds were collected. The bugle was sounded. The hunt *commenced*.

31. Jenny Lind sang her very best on that day. The audience *were* very much pleased.

32. He gave a very interesting and stirring address. The cause *was taken up* warmly by every one present.

33. The soldiers were seated round the bonfire. A man from the nearest village *provided* dinner.

34. The harvest had been gathered in. The rents were all paid. The usual festival *was held*.

35. The coast of Greece is almost entirely surrounded by sea. The neighbouring islands are very numerous. Piracy *was* much *practised* in ancient times.

36. There was a spare seat in the carriage. He *travelled* with me for some twenty miles.

37. The sun shone from the west. The clouds were gilded with light. The landscape *was* very beautiful.

38. The government was corrupt. The chief officials took bribes. Justice *was perverted* with impunity.

(c) *Combine the following sentences after the manner shown in* (c). *The Nominative and the Finite verb are indicated by Italics. But the student may choose any other Subject or Predicate that he prefers:—*

1. He drives a bullock cart. He carries goods from place to place. By this means *he earns* his living.

2. *He declined* to open his door to these visitors. He gave no reason for his refusal.

3. *The accused* had the right to challenge the jury. He *insisted* on this right.

4. The *men made* very little profit. Their industry was useless.

5. The *workmen are divided* into three different sets. One set excavates the clay. A second wheels it away in a wheelbarrow. The third puts it into the shape of bricks.

6. *Their brother* disguised himself as a sailor. He *knocked* at the front door.

7. There was a sound of some one breathing heavily. His *attention was attracted.*

8. There was an old Greek fable about king Midas. *Every thing* touched by him *turned* into gold.

9. The people crowded the streets to see him. His *progress was* very much *impeded.*

10. Columbus discovered America. A new *outlet was* thus *given* to European navigation and commerce.

11. The *king* and *queen* heard Columbus's story. They *fell* on their knees. They thus showed their gratitude to God. God had protected the traveller.

12. The *soldier appeared* on the scene. He had a bayonet in his right hand. The bayonet was held over his shoulder.

13. He was an eloquent speaker. *He was* also a successful man of business.

14. The annual festival was about to be held. The *lord* of the manor *invited* all his tenants.

15. *Romulus and Remus were suckled* by a she-wolf. Such was the legend of ancient Rome.

16. *The ancient Britons* had long been disused to war. They *were* easily *conquered* by the Saxons. The Romans had by this time departed.

17. The sun had set. The *travellers did* not *return.*

18. The *traveller returned* in safety from the Arctic seas. His friends were much relieved.

19. A new Triple *alliance was formed.* England, the United States, and Japan were parties to it.

20. The *ape was dressed* up like a soldier. The spectators were much amused.

21. The *dwarf* armed as a constable *ordered* the prince to go away. His manner was very humorous.

22. The *parents took* a great deal of trouble. They wished to make every child happy as well as useful.

23. That morning *I met* a woodman. He had an axe on his shoulder. He carried a rope in his left hand.

24. The *ship sailed* gaily along in a bright sunshine. The breeze rippled the surface of the sea.

25. The *traveller* decided to allow the robbers to search him. He did not resist.

26. The *victory* of Drake *dealt* a deadly blow. The power of Spain fell.

27. He leaped down from the window into the street. *He broke* his leg.

28. Being very sad *we travelled* along in silence. We never exchanged even a single word. We never got up from our seats till the journey's end.

29. The *Duke* of Wellington *was* a distinguished general. What especially made him distinguished was his coolness in the face of danger.

30. The *defenders* of Lucknow *felt* relieved at last. They had heard the bagpipe of Haveloc's Highlanders.

31. *The man* was visiting some friends in Yorkshire. He there *saw* the magnificent minster. This was the first time he had seen it.

32. The *battle* of Waterloo *was* decisive. It crushed the power of Napoleon.

33. The *legend* of the siege of Troy *has been handed* down. The great poets of ancient Greece have handed it down. It has been the delight of all ages and all countries.

34. The great conqueror *raised* his voice to speak. His heart was beating. His voice was trembling.

35. A great victory had been won in the East. All his countrymen *were* proud of it.

36. *He had been* very successful. All his plans prospered. All his projects turned out well.

37. His friends persuaded him. His enemies reproved him. *He yielded* at last.

(d) Combine the following sentences after the manner shown in (d). The Nominative and the Finite verb are indicated by Italics. But the student can adopt any other Subject or Predicate that he may prefer.

1. In such a matter as this there *is* only one *way*. By that you may succeed.

2. *He has* now fifteen pupils in his class. He must teach them. He must prepare them for the next examination.

3. *He had* no money left. He could not carry on the business any longer.

4. He desired to pay up all his creditors in full. *He made* arrangements for this purpose.

5. *The builder sold* all his plant. The paying of his creditors what he owed them was his motive.

6. *England maintains* a very great navy. Her Colonial and Indian empires need protection.

7. The planets revolve in certain orbits. *The planets have been observed* by astronomers.

8. Oliver Cromwell was declared a usurper. The Royalist *party* declared this.

9. *He drew up* his forces in battle array. The enemy were marching towards him. He had to meet them.

10. *He stayed* at home. He looked after his aged parents. This was his reason for staying there.

11. *The merchant* decided on getting his goods carried across the desert. He *hired* a dozen camels for this purpose.

12. Newton was the greatest of astronomers. *He is acknowledged* everywhere in this character.

13. A tired man enjoys the fresh breezes of the sea. *It is* very good for his health.

14. The skull bone protects the brain from harm. It *was made* hard for this purpose.

15. He did his duty in all things to the best of his power. His *zeal and earnestness were* very commendable.

16. *He must sign* his name. Otherwise the cheque will not be cashed.

17. *He must confess* his fault. Otherwise he will be fined.

18. He should make the best use of the short time left to him. My *advice* to him *was* this.

19. The sailors allowed no rats to be killed on the ship. *It was* their custom.

20. The *pigeons flew down.* They wished to pick up the grains. They wish to satisfy their hunger.

21. I wish to come to the point at once. *I cannot* keep you any longer in my service.

22. He was unable to teach such a large number of subjects to such a large class. *He had* not sufficient energy. He had not sufficient knowledge.

23. Every *company* of soldiers *has* a captain. He directs their movements. He watches their interests. He maintains discipline.

24. *He was* ill. For this reason he could not go to school on that day.

25. He wished to take a few days' holiday. *He petitioned* the officer.

26. We may give to the needy. We may receive a gift. *I would* rather do the former.

27. *The mice held* a meeting. Its object was to find out some way of thwarting the cat.

28. *The boy laughed.* He found himself caught in his own trap.

(*e*) *Combine the following sentences after the manner shown in* (*e*) :—

1. *He fled* from his creditors. This was a very dishonest act.

2. *Lord Clive* was formerly a writer in a merchant's office at Madras. He *founded* the British Empire in India.

3. *Cromwell assumed* the powers of a king. He had once been a private gentleman. Next he was a popular leader in the Long Parliament. Then he was commander of the Parliamentary forces. Finally, he was called Lord High Protector.

4. *Oliver Cromwell was succeeded* by his son. His son's name was Richard.

5. *Thomas Cromwell* was of a family quite distinct from that of Oliver Cromwell. He had been in Cardinal Wolsey's service. He became the secretary of Henry VIII. in A.D. 1530. He was executed by order of Henry VIII. in A.D. 1540.

6. *Bombala* is situated in New South Wales. It is a seaport with a twofold bay. It *is* at present first favourite as the site for the Federal capital of the Commonwealth of Australia.

7. There *is* yet another *article* concerning Stanislas. This Stanislas was the father of Louis XV.'s queen.

8. *Suraj-ud-Daulah* was viceroy of Bengal under the emperor of Delhi. He *shut-up* his prisoners in the Black Hole. This was a suffocating dungeon in Calcutta.

9. This *viceroy* perpetrated many atrocities. He oppressed the British merchants of Calcutta. He oppressed his own people no less. He *was defeated* at Plassey. This was a fit end to such an evil reign.

10. Beside him *sported* on the green his little granddaughter. Her name was Wilhelmine.

11. *You* are the writer of that libel. You *will suffer* the penalty. This will be a fit return for your malice.

12. That *law* has caused us a great deal of trouble. It has produced much discontent. It *must* be repealed at no distant date.

13. *Washington* is the federal capital of the United States. It *is called* after General Washington. He led the forces of the American colonies. He founded the great American Republic.

14. *Brutus conspired* with Cassius and others to put Julius Cæsar to death. Brutus was the enemy of kingly government of every form and kind. Julius Cæsar was the first man to make himself emperor of Rome. He was the first citizen to acquire an absolute power equal to that of a king.

15. *Sir Isaac Newton* discovered the motions of the heavenly bodies. *Locke* was the learned author of the "Human Understanding." They *flourished* at the same time.

16. *He has* many of the qualities of a great commander. He has coolness of judgment in sudden emergencies. He has skill in directing the movements of troops. He has foresight in anticipating the probable movements of his enemies.

17. *A. entered* into partnership with B. A. possessed a great deal of money still uninvested. B. possessed a great deal of knowledge and skill still unemployed. It was a fortunate union of diverse, but not conflicting, interests.

18. *John Bunyan wrote* a well-known book. It is called the *Pilgrim's Progress.* It is an allegory describing the trials and temptations of a Christian on his way to the Land of Promise. He had once been a thoughtless youth. Afterwards he became a religious penitent.

19. *Charles I.* was the second of the Stuarts. He firmly believed in the divine right of kings. He *aroused* the hostility of his subjects. He aroused especially the hostility of two celebrated men. These were Hampden

and Cromwell. The former was the champion of popular rights against illegal taxation. The latter became the leader of the Parliamentary forces.

SECTION 2.—TO COMBINE SIMPLE SENTENCES INTO A COMPOUND SENTENCE

56. Compound Sentence.—A compound sentence is one that consists of two or more mutually independent clauses; that is, of clauses which are combined by Co-ordinative conjunctions, or by phrases that have the force of such conjunctions.

Co-ordinative conjunctions differ from one another in sense. Some, such as "*and*," express merely the *addition* of one statement to another. Others, such as "*but*," express a *contrast* between one statement and another. Others again, such as *for* or *therefore*, express an *inference* of one statement from another. So, when two or more simple sentences are given and the student is required to combine them into one Compound sentence, he must consider in what sense or relation, whether of addition, or of contrast, or of inference, one statement stands to another, and select the conjunction accordingly.

The different modes of combination will be seen from the following examples:—

(*a*) *By using some conjunction that expresses addition*:—

Separate. I worked hard. I gained a prize.
Combined. I worked hard *and* (I) gained a prize.

(*b*) *By using some conjunction that expresses contrast*:—

Separate. He is poor. He is contented.
Combined. He is poor, *but* (he is) contented.

(*c*) *By using some conjunction that expresses inference*:—

Separate. He is not a happy man. He has bad health.
Combined. He is not a happy man; *for* he has bad health.

(*d*) *By using two or more conjunctions that have different values*:—

Separate. I will lay me down in peace. I will sleep. Thou, Lord, only makest me dwell in safety.
Combined. I will *both* lay me down in peace, *and* sleep: *for* thou, Lord, only makest me dwell in safety.—*Psalms* iv. 8.

Note on Co-ordinative conjunctions and their equivalents.

(*a*) The chief conjunctions expressing the addition of one statement to another are the following:—

And.—One received praise, *and* the other censure.

(This is the simplest and most frequently used conjunction of the class.)

Both . . . and.—He is *both* a fool *and* a knave.

(This pair gives emphasis to the fact that the two statements are united. Generally speaking, a fool is one kind of man and a knave is another. To show that the two characters may be united in the same person, we use *both . . . and*.

Not only . . . but also.—He was *not only* degraded to a lower class, *but* was expelled from the school.

(The more emphatic statement is placed last.)

As well as.—He was expelled *as well as* degraded.

(The more emphatic statement is placed first.)

Firstly . . . secondly, etc.; **now . . . then**; **here . . . there**; **on this side . . . on that side**; **partly . . . partly.**—These adverbs or adverbial phrases have a conjunctive force, since they join one statement to another by way of addition or continuation.

Where, when, whence, who, whom, which, whose.

—A Relative pronoun or Relative adverb, when it is used in the sense of merely adding one statement to another, has the force of a co-ordinative conjunction.

Separate. We landed at Calcutta. We stopped *there* for a week.
Combined. We landed at Calcutta, *where* (=and there) we stopped for a week.

Separate. They sent Mr. A. as messenger. He explained the matter.
Combined. They sent Mr. A. as messenger, *who* (=and he) explained the matter.

(*b*) The chief conjunctions expressing a contrast between one statement or fact and another are the following:—

But.—He is poor, *but* contented.

(This is the chief conjunction of the class. Poverty is not usually combined with contentment. So *but* is the appropriate conjunction for uniting the two statements.)

But then, still, yet, however.—These have the same force as *but.* But they throw a little more emphasis than "but" on the second clause; and when these are used, the second clause is generally written out in full.

Separate. He did not get the first place. He was much praised for his zeal and energy.
Combined. He did not get the first place; *still* (or *but then* or *yet*) he was much praised for his zeal and energy. Or, he was much praised, *however*, for his zeal and energy.

Nevertheless; at the same time.—These phrases have a powerful effect in setting one statement against another. They have much the same force as the preceding.

On the one hand . . . on the other hand.—These phrases are used to balance one fact or argument against another. That fact or argument, to which the greater importance is attached, is mentioned last. The last is meant to outweigh the first.

Separate. There were very strong suspicions against him. The facts disclosed by the witnesses all told in his favour.

Combined. *On the one hand* there were very strong suspicions against him; *on the other* the facts disclosed by the witnesses all told in his favour.

Only.—This is properly an adverb; but it has a conjunctional force, when it is meant to express an exception or contrast to some general statement or order.

Separate. Go wherever you like. Do not stop here.
Combined. Go wherever you like; *only* do not stop here.

(*c*) The chief conjunctions expressing an inference of one statement from another are **for** and **therefore.** A weaker inference is expressed by **so**:—

Separate. Cricket is the grandest of school games. Every boy should learn it.

Combined. Cricket is the grandest of school games, and therefore every boy should learn it.

or Every boy should learn cricket; for it is the grandest of school games.

Observe, when *therefore* is used, the reason is given in the first sentence, and the inference in the second; but when *for* is used, the inference is given in the first sentence, and the reason in the second.

So, then, hence, consequently.—These are other modes of expressing *therefore*. *So*, *hence*, *consequently*, are often, like *therefore*, preceded by "and."

Exercise on § 56. (To be done orally and at sight.[1])

Combine the following sentences by some Co-ordinative conjunction or Conjunctional phrase, according to

[1] *To Teacher.*—If students should find it rather difficult to combine these sentences at sight on first trial, they will find that it comes easier by practice. It might also be advisable for them to do their exercise twice over, and to write out some of the examples (in their combined form) both for purposes of revision and as a lesson in penmanship.

the sense or relation in which one sentence stands to the other or others :—

1. They could not decide the point themselves. They asked a third person to decide it for them.
2. The fear of the Lord is the beginning of knowledge. The foolish despise wisdom.
3. Refrain thy foot from their path. Their feet run to evil. They make haste to shed blood.
4. They despised my warning. They shall eat of the fruit of their own way.
5. In all thy ways acknowledge Him. He shall direct thy paths.
6. Honour the Lord with thy substance. Thy horns shall be filled with plenty.
7. Her ways are ways of pleasantness. All her paths are peace.
8. The curse of the Lord is in the house of the wicked. He blesseth the habitation of the righteous.
9. He scorneth the scorners. He giveth grace unto the lowly.
10. Exalt wisdom. She shall promote thee.
11. Blessed are the meek. They shall inherit the earth.
12. Blessed are the merciful. They shall obtain mercy.
13. The sluggard will not plough by reason of the toil. He shall beg in the harvest. He shall have nothing.
14. He is a rich man. He is not proud of his wealth. He makes no distinction between rich and poor.
15. The feet of a cat are furnished with long sharp claws. A bird or mouse, once caught, cannot escape.
16. An honest man will speak out. He will not be afraid of the consequences.
17. A timid man may conceal the truth. By speaking the truth he is afraid of some harm coming to him.
18. In all labour there is profit. The talk of the lips tends only to penury.
19. He was said to have been taken seriously ill. He was quite well. He was doing his work, as usual, yesterday.

20. In private life he was amiable and gentle. In public life he was severe. He attended to all his duties most carefully.

21. He was walking along alone one night. He met a thoughtless young fellow. This young fellow would not move out of his way to let him pass.

22. The son of Henry IV., the Prince of Wales, had a strong sense of justice. He knew the duties of a subject. He was quick-tempered. On one occasion he struck Sir W. Gascoigne, a judge. Sir W. was at that time seated in the bench.

23. Sir W. Gascoigne knew the dignity and power of his position. He resolved to do his duty at all hazards. He instantly ordered the Prince of Wales to be committed to prison.

24. Life has few enjoyments. We cling to it.

25. They died on the battle-field. They lay on a bed of honour.

26. At this time of the year I do not rise at five o'clock in the morning. I rise at seven or eight.

27. He was clever, accomplished, and possessed of every virtue. He was of a timid disposition.

28. You made a deplorable mistake. It was done in ignorance. You deserve to be pardoned.

29. We must reach Brighton by four o'clock. There is only one hour left. We must start at once.

30. He received all the pay promised him. He was dissatisfied. He took the case into court.

31. Cast thy bread upon the waters. Thou shalt find it after many days.

32. It was too late to start on our journey. We postponed starting till the following morning.

33. The people of this place are industrious. They are thrifty. I noticed the crops standing in the fields. I noticed the neatness of the cottages.

34. Not only have I done wrong. You also have done wrong. You attempted to gain a certificate on false pretences.

35. The prince with all his wealth was jealous of the

hermit. The hermit's reputation was superior to the prince's.

36. A large number of the wounded recovered. They took up arms again in the following year. They wished to defend the country. They loved the country.

37. The boat seemed likely to sink. He did not lose courage. He brought the boat safely to land.

38. He caught the robbers. He never got back the stolen property. The property consisted of gold and silver ornaments.

39. In full armour the barons attended a council at Westminster. At Westminster they demanded a redress of their grievances.

40. That cave was said to contain many curious relics. We could not enter it. We had no torches. It would have been dangerous to enter it in the dark.

41. Edward now proceeded to Calais. From Calais he crossed over to Dover.

42. Robert Bruce took advantage of Edward's absence. He invaded England. He was king of Scotland. He was the ally of France.

43. The northern states of America had a contest with the southern. The contest lasted four years. It ended in the defeat and surrender of the southern states.

44. The government of Henry III. was as unpopular as that of King John. He had foreign favourites. He levied unjust taxes. The nobles were determined to put an end to these things.

45. The king spent the following year in Normandy. In Normandy he desired to strengthen his position. He desired to secure the succession of his son.

46. He always prepared his lessons to the best of his power. Through no fault of his own, he did not reach a high place in the class. He was not naturally clever.

47. In the last years of his life, Henry I.'s great object in life was to secure the crown for his only daughter, Matilda. Prince William, his only son, had been drowned.

48. The tanks were dry. The fields could not be

irrigated. A visitation of famine was certain. The annual rains had failed.

49. Enter not into the path of the wicked. Go not in the way of evil men. They eat the bread of wickedness. They drink the wine of violence.

Section 3.—To combine Simple Sentences into a Complex Sentence[1]

57. Complex sentence.—A Complex sentence is one that consists of a Principal clause (that is, the clause containing the main *verb* of the sentence) with one or more Subordinate or Dependent clauses:—

Complex { A merchant, who had much property to sell, *caused* all his goods to be conveyed on camels, as there was no railroad in that country.

Simple { A merchant, having much property to sell, *caused* all his goods to be conveyed on camels, there being no railroad in that country.

The two sentences mean precisely the same thing, and both have a Finite verb in common, *caused*. But in other respects they are entirely different. In the latter there is but *one* Finite verb, *caused*, and therefore the sentence is Simple. In the former, besides the Finite verb *caused*, there are two more Finite verbs, *had* and *was*; and therefore the sentence cannot be Simple, but must be either Compound or Complex.

The sentence is not Compound, but Complex, because—(1) The clause "who had much property to sell" is connected with the noun "merchant," which it qualifies as an adjective would do; and (2) the

[1] *To Teacher.*—The suggestions offered in footnote 1 to § 55 are intended to apply to the working of the Examples given in this section, and also to those given in Section 4.

clause "as there was no railroad in that country" is connected with the verb "caused," which it qualifies as an adverb would do. Neither of these clauses can stand alone; neither of them gives an independent sense without reference to some outside word; and hence the sentence, as a whole, cannot be Compound. There is one Principal or Containing clause, and two Subordinate or Contained clauses. The sentence is therefore Complex.

58. Noun-clause.—A noun-clause is so called, because it *does the work of a noun.* It may be the subject of a verb (as a noun may be); or the object of a verb (as a noun may be); or the object of a preposition (as a noun may be); or the complement of a verb (as a noun may be); or in apposition with a noun (as a noun may be):—

Who steals my purse steals trash .	*Subj. of verb.*
I shall be glad to know *when you will return*	*Obj. of verb.*
This will sell for *what it is worth* .	*Obj. of prep.*
This is exactly *what I expected* .	*Compl. of verb.*
The rumour *that he is sick* is false .	*App. to noun.*

From the above examples it will be seen that a Noun-clause can be introduced either by the conjunction *that,* or by a Relative pronoun (having no antecedent), or by a Relative adverb, such as *when, where, whence, how, why* (no antecedent being expressed).

Exercise on § 58. (To be done orally and at sight.)

Combine the following Simple sentences into a Complex sentence, containing a Noun-clause. The main verb is indicated by italics:—

1. He will come at some time or other. No one *knows* the time.

2. By some means or other this has come to pass. The means *is* not known to any one.

3. Rain will fall to-day. This *is* quite evident.

4. The air is never quite at rest. You *must* know this.

5. I shall never clearly understand this. So I *think*.

6. The school will open in ten days' time. So we *heard*.

7. The burning hills of the Mediterranean were the workshops of the divine blacksmith, Vulcan. That was the belief of the ancient Greeks. The name "Volcano" *indicates* this belief.

8. The wind is blowing in a certain direction. Even a feather *shows* the direction.

9. His father had been shot. He *did* not know it.

10. You have not signed your name to a letter. This *shows* your character. You lack moral courage.

11. Even the simplest weapons were useful to the first dwellers on the earth. This *will* be easily understood.

12. How is fire to be made? This *is* the question first occurring to the mind of a savage.

13. Fire can be produced by rubbing two sticks together. Common sense soon *taught* him this.

14. In the chipping of flint-weapons fire occasionally flashes out. The first men *must* have seen this.

15. Savages can produce fire in a few seconds. We *learn* this from travellers.

16. He says something. We *cannot* rely on it.

17. You have made a mistake. This *is* quite evident.

18. You were taken ill. This *was* very unfortunate.

19. He *was* a man of fine character in all points except one. He was rather timid.

20. What do you desire to have? I *will grant* you anything.

21. We can make our lives sublime. Lives of great men all *remind* us of this.

22. He cannot resist your claims. He cannot deny your merits. Of this you *may* be sure.

23. A certain amount of time is required for preparing plans. You *shall* be granted it in full.

24. The messenger told you something about that matter. I *heard* it.

25. It was your duty to make the best use of your time at school. You *found* out this too late.

26. Your hopes about your son's future may or may not be fulfilled. Time alone *will* show.

27. Columbus discovered America in a certain way. He was provided with ships and men by a certain king. He met with certain difficulties in the way. *Tell* me about the way, the king, and the difficulties.

28. The Russians, in the Crimean war, remained strictly on the defensive. It *is* not difficult to perceive the reason.

29. I have seen that man's face before somewhere. I *cannot* now remember the place.

30. You have come from a certain place. You have come for a certain purpose. You began your journey on a certain day. You arrived here on a certain day. I *should like* to be told the place, the purpose, and the days.

31. The earth moves round the sun. The sun does not move round the earth. Astronomers *have* clearly proved this.

32. The excessive heat at Sandhurst in the summer of 1900, and the number of deaths from sunstroke during the review, *gave* rise to two questions—Should a review have been held at all in such weather? If so, should not the heads of the men be better protected?

59. Adjective clause.—An adjective clause is so called, because it *does the work of an adjective;* that is, it qualifies some noun as an adjective would do.

An adjective clause is introduced by a Relative pronoun or a Relative adverb. The noun that stands as antecedent to the Relative pronoun or Relative adverb is the noun qualified by the adjective clause:—

A man *who has just come* inquired after you.
This is not the book *that I selected.*
This is not such a horse *as I should have chosen.*
We found it in the place *where we left it.*

Exercise on § 59. (To be done orally and at sight.)

Combine the following sentences into a Complex sentence, containing an adjective clause. The main verb is indicated by italics :—

1. The theft was committed. The time of its commission *was* never found out.
2. The theft was committed. The man *has* been caught.
3. We lived in a house. The house *has* fallen down.
4. This *is* the story. I heard it ten years ago.
5. I should have chosen a certain kind of book. This *is* not such a one.
6. He *made* his living by getting presents. He received these presents from certain men. He had long served such men.
7. Man *has* the power of making certain instruments. Such instruments bring stars into view. The light of those stars has taken a thousand years to reach the earth.
8. Men now *catch* the reanimated fish in ponds. From those ponds, but a week before, the wind blew clouds of dust.
9. At different parts of its course a river *is entered* by tributaries. These tributaries swell its waters.
10. Of what use *is* a knowledge of books to him? He fails to practise virtue.
11. Fortune *selects* a certain kind of man for her friend. Such a man reflects before acting.
12. Springs *are fed* by rain. The rain has percolated into the earth through crevices in rock or soil.
13. Shakspeare was born in a certain house. I *have seen* it.
14. You acted on a certain plan. It *has answered* well.
15. You are telling me a certain story. Surely it *is* not true.
16. Such a man *is* thrice armed. He has his quarrel just.
17. Nancoomar *prepared* to die with quiet fortitude. With such fortitude the Bengalee, so backward as a rule in personal conflict, often encounters the direst calamities. There is no escape from them.

18. The Saxon and Danish dialects *were* different forms of a certain language. This language was once widely spoken in northern Europe.

19. Every one spoke well of that man thirty years ago. He was then a fine young cricketer. Now he *has become* a confirmed drunkard.

20. One of the great annual fairs is held at Muttra. Muttra is visited on that occasion by many pilgrims from all parts of India. Muttra *is* one of the most ancient cities of Hindustan.

21. A small rest-house stood at the foot of the hill. We *stopped* there for the night.

22. The shipwrecked mariners *watched* for the ship. On the approach of this ship all their hopes of rescue were centred.

23. He had received a good education. This *raised* him above many men of his own age and rank.

24. In our ramble through the forest we *came* upon a thatched cottage. A fine cedar tree was growing by its side. The tree stood forty or fifty feet high.

25. He has no money laid by. He cannot borrow. He cannot even earn a decent income. A man of that kind *is* rather to be pitied.

26. The Indian Empire was acquired by the British in various ways. He briefly *described* the most important of these to the audience.

27. I *went* down a footpath. At the end of the footpath there was a chasm forty feet deep. The dead body of a man was lying there. A faithful dog was still seated by its side.

60. Adverb-clause.—An Adverb-clause is so called because it *does the work of an adverb*; that is, it qualifies some verb, adjective, or other adverb in the same way as an adverb itself would qualify it. Those conjunctions, which are used for introducing an Adverb clause, are called Subordinative.

Subordinative conjunctions differ from one another

according to sense. So when a Principal sentence is given, and one or more other Simple sentences have to be combined with it as Subordinate clauses, the student must consider in what sense or relation the Subordinate clause or clauses are intended to stand to the Principal clause, and select the conjunction accordingly.

(*a*) *Cause* or *Reason*: the chief conj. are **because, since, as.**

Separate. He will succeed. He has worked hard.
Combined. He will succeed, *because* or *since* or *as* he has worked hard.

(*b*) *Effect*: the chief conj. is **that.**

Separate. He worked hard. He made himself ill.
Combined. He worked *so* hard, *that* he made himself ill.

(*c*) *Purpose*: the chief conj. are **that, in order that, so that, lest.**

Separate. Men work. They wish to earn a living.
Combined. Men work, *that* or *so that* they may earn a living.

Separate. He walked with care. He did not wish to fall.
Combined. He walked with care, *lest* he should fall.

(*d*) *Conditions*: the chief conj. are **if, unless, provided.**

Separate. I will do this. My being allowed is a condition.
Combined. I will do this, *if* or *provided* I am allowed.

Separate. I will go. My not being prevented is a condition.
Combined. I will go, *unless* I am prevented.

(*e*) *Concession* or *Contrast*: the chief conj. are **though, as, however.**

Separate. He is contented. He is poor.
Combined. He is contented, *although* he is poor.
Poor *as* he is, he is contented.
However poor he is, he is contented.

(*f*) *Comparison* (1) *of equal degrees:* the chief conj. are **as—as, as much as.**

Separate. He is clever. His cleverness equals mine.
Combined. He is *as* clever *as* I am.

Separate. He likes you. His liking for you equals mine.
Combined. He likes you *as much as* I do.

(*g*) *Comparison* (2) *of unequal degrees:* the conj. is **than.**

Separate. He is more clever. I am less clever.
Combined. He is more clever *than* I am.

(*h*) *Extent* or *Manner:* the chief conj. are **as, so far as.**

Separate. Men may sow much or little, wisely or unwisely. They will reap accordingly.
Combined. Men will reap *as* they sow.

Separate. I will tell you to the extent of my knowledge. The extent of my knowledge may be small or great.
Combined. I will tell you *so far as* I know.

(*i*) *Time simultaneous:* the chief conj. are **as, as soon as, when.**

Separate. He was very sorry. He found out his mistake.
Combined. He was very sorry, *when* he found out his mistake.

Separate. The bell rang. They all immediately came up.
Combined. *As soon as* the bell rang, they all came up.

(*j*) *Time during:* the chief conj. are **while, so long as.**

Separate. Life still remains. There is hope.
Combined. *While* or *so long as* there is life, there is hope.

(*k*) *Time before:* the chief conj. is **before.**

Separate. I refuse to pay at present. You must give me a receipt.
Combined. *Before* I consent to pay, you must give me a receipt.

(*l*) *Time up to:* the conj. is **till** or **until.**

Separate. He remained a minor. He was not yet twenty-one.
Combined. He remained a minor, *till* he was twenty-one.

(*m*) *Time after:* the conj. are **after, since.**

Separate. He returned home. He had finished the work.
Combined. He returned home, *after* he had finished the work.

Separate. He was taken ill. He has been weak from that time.
Combined. He has been weak, *since* he was taken ill.

Exercise on § 60. (To be done orally and at sight.)

Combine the following sentences into a Complex sentence containing an Adverb-clause. The main verb is indicated by italics:—

1. Men *engage* in some work. They wish to earn a living.
2. They *threatened* to beat him. The beating would be given for not confessing his fault.
3. He *was* always contented and happy. Yet he was poor.
4. He *likes* you up to a certain point. I like you to the same extent.
5. He *tried* for a long time. At last he succeeded.

6. It is now late. *Let* us go to bed.
7. He *walked* with care. He was afraid of stumbling.
8. I *agree* to this. But you must sign your name.
9. He may punish me. Yet *will* I trust in him.
10. He *returned* home. He had finished the work.
11. *Prove* a friend. Then trust him.
12. He *persevered* steadily. Success was the result.
13. I *will* let this man off. He has been well punished already.
14. He is sixty years old. Yet his eyesight *is* excellent.
15. I *gave* him a prize. Under that inducement he might work harder next year.
16. They *deserted* their former associate. He had become poor and unfortunate.
17. The tree falls in a certain way. In that way it *will* lie.
18. We left the house at a certain time. It *has* not ceased raining ever since that time.
19. I *should* be glad to lend you that money. I have not as much in my own pocket.
20. Murder has no tongue. Yet it *will* speak.
21. You must leave the house at once. I *will* send for a policeman.
22. Ambassadors *were sent* from Sparta. Their mission was to sue for peace.
23. He *left off* even trying to do his best. He could not give satisfaction.
24. He *must be* very tired. He had no sleep last night.
25. All men must die and be forgotten. Why then *does* he seek for fame and riches?
26. He *learnt* Euclid rapidly. In so doing he astonished his teachers.
27. He *gave* up most of his spare time to home preparation. He wished to gain a scholarship at the end of the term.
28. A thief *does* his work very cautiously. He does not wish to be caught in the act.

29. I may perhaps be allowed to speak. I *am* ready to explain everything.

30. The rain may fall this month. With the fall of rain there *will* be no fear of famine.

31. He should be very careful. Without care he *will* come to serious harm.

32. He may give me leave. He may not give me leave. I *shall* go back to my parents in either case.

33. He became more and more rich. He *was* never contented.

34. He has been very unfortunate. Yet he *is* always cheerful.

35. R. *is* a lazy boy. The other boys in the class are not equally lazy.

36. R. *is* a clever boy. No other boy in the class is more clever.

37. The branches of some trees *grow* to a great height. The roots are equally deep.

38. Men may do well or ill in this life. They *will* be blessed or miserable to the same extent hereafter.

39. India has fallen under British rule. It *has* always been free from external attack from that time.

40. The judge has already decided the case. Further defence *is* useless.

41. Her son has escaped from many dangers. The mother sees it. She *is* much consoled in seeing it.

42. He *spoke* rapidly. We could not clearly understand him.

43. He did not consent to ride that spirited horse. He *was* not so courageous.

44. The trick was found out. The master *ordered* the man to be expelled from the house at once.

45. He *made* an excellent speech in defence of his friend. Every one admired him in consequence. Every one respected him.

46. The reasons of this unfortunate result *are* complicated. I am unable to explain them at once.

47. The success of that dull boy in the last examination *was* unexpected. Suspicions were roused.

SECTION 4.—THE FORMATION OF MIXED SENTENCES.

61. Mixed Sentences.—We often meet with a sentence which consists of two Co-ordinate clauses, and is therefore Compound: but each Co-ordinate clause contains one or more Subordinate clauses. Such sentences are Mixed, partly Compound and partly Complex.

What is obvious is not always known, and what is known is not always present.

Here we have four Finite verbs and therefore four clauses. The sentence as a whole is Compound, the two parts being combined co-ordinately by *and*. But each part contains a Subordinate clause. "What is obvious" is a Noun-clause in the first part; and "what is known" is a Noun-clause in the second. Two Complex sentences are thus joined together by a Co-ordinative conjunction so as to make one Compound sentence.

Exercise on § 61. (To be done orally and at sight.)

Combine the following Simple sentences in any way that may seem to come most easily or make the best result, whether the result be a Simple, or a Compound, or a Complex, or a Mixed sentence. The main verb is indicated by Italics.

1. He had enormous wealth. He never *enjoyed* peace of mind. He never enjoyed health of body.
2. He made some foolish remarks. They related to an event in his past life. He *was* not on his guard at the time of making them.
3. You stand to me in a certain relation at present. This relation *may* be reversed at some future time. The time may not be very distant.

4. His kindness to me *has been* of such a character. I cannot express it. He could not increase it. I never did anything to deserve it.

5. *Let* us take a walk into the grove. The grove is now thickly strewn with fallen leaves.

6. Hannibal led an army against Rome. The army *was* very formidable. Up to that time the Romans had not encountered an army so formidable.

7. The man *disguised* himself. He painted his face. He dyed his hair. He put on a strange coat.

8. My friend is an excellent rider. His horse played him many tricks. In spite of these tricks he *managed* to keep his seat.

9. The English nation *honours* the name of Wellington. He won the battle of Waterloo. He won many other great battles in the service of his country.

10. Affairs took a certain course after the 24th May. By this course the whole plan *was upset*. The upsetting was unavoidable and beyond recovery.

11. Their forefathers displayed high examples of courage in a previous age. Men *should strive* to imitate such examples. They should strive to bequeath similar examples to their posterity.

12. We decided on building a cottage in the vale. The vale *is* watered by a streamlet. The streamlet flows from a perennial fountain.

13. By the waters of Babylon the Jews *sat down* and wept. They remembered Sion. From Sion they had been taken captive.

14. Ghosts *were seen* to walk in the streets of Rome. This is according to the legend then current. Julius Cæsar was murdered at that time.

15. He *left* the house in great anger. He had taken offence at certain remarks. The last speaker had made them.

16. The fire was put out. The inmates of the house were rescued. The firemen then *removed* the pumps. They desired to take a little rest.

17. The signal was given. Every one immediately

raised a shout. They desired by so doing to give a hearty welcome to the royal visitor.

18. What evils *have befallen* him? Why should he be so much pitied by every one?

19. Any branch of knowledge can be conquered by perseverance. There *is* no branch of knowledge too difficult for this.

20. The rope in your hand must have a stone tied to the end of it. It will touch the bottom of the well. It *is* long enough for this purpose.

21. The first shower of rain had fallen. The peasant at once *brought* his oxen and plough. He desired to break the first sod. He desired to cast the first seed into the earth.

22. He worked patiently and industriously. I saw it. I immediately *decided* to give him some pecuniary help.

23. The traveller enters the Suez Canal. Some rocks first meet his eye. These *are* a part of a breakwater. This breakwater was built for some two miles out into the sea. Ships may thus enter the canal in safety.

24. A ship is sometimes accidentally grounded in the Suez Canal. At such times great delays *are caused*. All other vessels are then detained. That ship has to be removed. The way has to be cleared for other ships to pass.

25. Formerly the canal had not been cut. Before that time, vessels bound for India *had* to proceed by a long and tedious voyage. They had to round the Cape of Good Hope. By rounding this Cape they might enter the waters of the Indian Ocean.

26. The Suez Canal *is* not likely to be obstructed or closed. Treaties have been signed between the principal nations of Europe. These provide against the occurrence of war. Even in time of war all vessels shall be permitted to pass unhindered.

27. You are now well acquainted with the facts. You *can* judge for yourself. Have I been fairly or not fairly treated in this question? To its consideration I had given much time and labour.

28. The weather was bad. It threatened to become

worse and worse. We *stayed* at home. We did not desire to be drenched with rain. Our journey was not yet finished.

29. He *is* miserable now. In his youth he was idle. He was self-indulgent. He placed no restraint upon his passions. He neglected his opportunities.

30. He *would* have come to a miserable end. A stranger unexpectedly appeared. This stranger relieved him of his most urgent wants.

31. I was thoroughly acquainted with his designs. I knew his character. Otherwise he *would* have brought me into serious trouble.

32. The traveller was furnished with ample means. He had received the clearest instructions as to the course to be taken. Yet he *missed* his way. He took another road. This road led him a long way round.

33. A student may be ever so dull. A subject may seem to be ever so difficult at first. The student *will find* it become either easier or more difficult. This will depend on his own perseverance or neglect.

34. The Amir of Afghanistan *has written* a most interesting book. In it he tells the story of his own life. Part of his life was spent in banishment from his own country. In that country he is now absolute master. He labours night and day for its protection and improvement.

35. We *were* all much distressed at his words. We did not suspect him of speaking an untruth. We feared he had almost lost his senses.

36. The sailors *refused* to go on board. The ship was overloaded. A storm might at any time arise. The ship in this case would be unable to climb the waves.

37. What fault *has* he *committed?* Should he be dismissed in this way? Should he be sent away in disgrace?

38. His enemies *looked* upon him with suspicion. They were a powerful body. The expression of his face could not remove this suspicion. His promises could not remove it. His threats could not remove it.

39. The prisoner *was captured* by the police. They had pursued him for more than an hour.

40. The use of Latin lasted all through the Middle Ages. At last it *was given up* in favour of English. English was spoken by the masses. It was also found useful by statesmen and men of science.

41. He had led a laborious life. He had spent most of it in the metropolis. In his old age he *retired* to a quiet village. There he was born. There he desired to spend his remaining years.

CHAPTER V.—DIRECT AND INDIRECT SPEECH.

62. Direct and Indirect Speech.—A speech is said to be in *Direct* narrative when the very words used by the speaker are repeated without any change;—in *Indirect* narrative, when the main words are the same, but the construction is somewhat changed, and pronouns of the Third person are substituted for those of the First or Second.

63. Assertive Sentences.—When the speaker simply affirms or denies something, and his speech is expressed in the Indirect form, the tense of the verb in the reported speech is bound by the same rules as those given in § 54 for the "Sequence of Tenses," ch. iii.

Thus by Rule I., when the reporting or principal verb is in the Past tense, the Present tense in the reported speech must be changed to its corresponding Past form. Thus we change:—

Shall	into	*should.*	*See*	into	*saw.*
Will	,,	*would.*	*Is seeing*	,,	*was seeing.*
May	,,	*might.*	*Has seen*	,,	*had seen.*
Can	,,	*could.*	*Has been seeing*	,,	*had been seeing.*

Similarly, when the Present tense is changed into the

Past by Rule I., an adjective or adverb expressing *nearness* is changed into one expressing *distance*. Thus we usually have to change :—

Now	into	*then.*	*Hence*	into	*thence.*
This, these	,,	*that, those.*	*Thus*	,,	*so.*
Hither	,,	*thither.*	*To-day*	,,	*that day.*
Here	,,	*there.*	*Last night*	,,	*the previous night.*

On the other hand, by Rule II., when the reporting or principal verb is in a Present or a Future tense, the tense of the verb in the reported speech remains unchanged, nor is any change made in the adverbs of time or place, such as *now* into *then*, *here* into *there*.

Example of Rule I.—

Direct.—He said, "The man *shall now* come."
Indirect.—He said that the man *should then* come.

Example of Rule II.—

Direct.—He says, "The man *shall now* come."
Indirect.—He says that the man *shall now* come.

Exercises on § 63. (To be done orally and at sight.)

(*a*) *Convert the following from Direct to Indirect* :—

1. He said, "The man will be here soon."
2. The judge will say to you, "You are innocent."
3. He said, "Abundant rain fell yesterday, and is falling still."
4. All men declare, "He has never yet been defeated."
5. He has told them, "I did not commit this fault."
6. He is still declaring, "You are the man who did it."
7. He told them at once, "The train is gone ; you are too late."
8. The news was announced, "The conquering hero is coming."
9. They received notice, "You may all come."
10. He has been saying all day, "I am tired of work."
11. I shall tell him plainly, "You cannot come here again."

12. I told him plainly, "You can go to-morrow."

13. I shall always affirm, "He, not I, is the guilty man."

14. He repeated day after day, "This climate does not suit my health; I must go away as soon as I can."

15. We told him, "The weather is stormy and the way is long."

16. We were informed, "The carriage is ready; we shall have to get back before the clock strikes four."

17. Notice was put up, "The prizes awarded this term will be presented to-morrow."

18. He was privately informed, "Your fault will be pardoned, if you confess it without reserve."

19. The banker announced, "I will agree to what you propose, if you sign this document, and pay the usual fee."

20. The judge decides, "The man is guilty of murder, and will be hanged in four days' time."

21. The man has confessed, "I am the guilty man, and deserve the punishment."

22. And Jacob said, "It is enough; my son Joseph is yet alive; I will go and see him before I die."—*Old Test.*

23. And David's anger was greatly kindled, and he said, "The man who hath done this thing deserveth to die, and he shall restore the lamb fourfold."—*Old Test.*

(*b*) *Convert the following from Indirect to Direct:—*

1. He assured them that he would soon return.

2. He told them that he had been robbed of the book which he had bought.

3. He said he was very sorry for the fault he had committed.

4. They all said to him that he deserved to be pardoned.

5. They affirmed that he was the best worker they had seen.

6. He admitted that he had not worked so hard as A. had done.

7. He heard them say that he did not deserve the prize.

8. He made a promise that he would do it as soon as he could.

9. They said that he had deserved their thanks for all he had done.

10. All who heard this said that he was speaking the truth.

11. He said that he had been three years in jail and yet was innocent.

12. They told him they would never believe what he said.

13. He answered that he would prove what he said to be true.

14. My brother told me that he had been reading all day.

15. My father told me that I was wrong and would be fined.

16. I replied that if my fault were proved I would pay the fine.

17. I admitted that I had acted foolishly in what I said.

18. He told me that I was mistaken,—that I should not go after all.

19. He told me I might leave this place as soon as I could.

20. The cow left the dog lying in the manger, and went away saying that the dog could neither eat the hay himself nor would allow her to eat it.

21. A wolf seeing a she-goat grazing on the top of a high cliff, begged her to come down, and told her that the grass was much sweeter down below than up there, and that if she came down as he advised her, she would get a much better dinner.

22. The goat thanked him and said that she would not come down until he went away, as he was thinking more about his own dinner than about hers.

23. A man, being blamed for hanging a sheep, which in reality was a wolf in sheep's clothing, replied that he made it a rule to hang a wolf whenever he got one, although the wolf might be in the garb of a sheep, like that animal there.

64. Interrogative sentences.—When the reported speech contains a question, and not an assertion or denial, the verb "say" or "tell" by which it is introduced has to be changed to "ask" or "inquire":—

Direct. Coming up, he *said*, "What *is* the way to Oxford?"

Indirect. Coming up he *inquired* what *was* the way to Oxford.

65. Imperative sentences.—When the verb in the reported speech is in the Imperative mood, the verb going before has to be changed to some verb expressing a command, a precept, or an entreaty, and the verb in the reported speech must be changed from the Imperative mood to the Infinitive:—

Direct. He *said* to the student, "*Do* not *make* any noise."

Indirect. { He *forbade* the student *to make* any noise.
He *ordered* or *told* the student not *to make* any noise.

66. Exclamatory sentences.—When the reported speech expresses an exclamation, the verb going before must be changed to one that is best suited to the sense:—

Direct. He *said*, "*Alas!* how foolish I *have* been!"

Indirect. He *confessed with regret* that he *had* been very foolish.

Exercise on §§ 64-66. (To be done orally and at sight.)

Convert the following from Direct to Indirect:—

1. As he passed me he said, "Where are you going?"
2. He said to the messenger, "Start at once."
3. He said to them all, "Good-bye, my friends!"
4. With much earnestness he said, "May God forgive him!"
5. He turned to his friend and said, "Wait till I return."

6. He said to his friend, "Be so kind as to lend me that book ?"

7. Looking angrily at him he said, "Why do you stand here ?"

8. With much indignation he said, "Why did you strike me ?"

9. He will certainly say, "Have you been reading to-day or not ?"

10. In a tone of penitence he said, "Pardon me this once."

11. He exclaimed, "Hurrah ! my friend has come."

12. His advice to the boy was, "Work steadily ! fear nothing !"

13. And Reuben said unto them, "Shed no blood ; cast Joseph into this pit that is in the wilderness, but lay no hand on him."—*Old Test.*

14. And Judah said unto his brethren, "What profit is it, if we slay our brother and conceal his blood ? Come, let us sell him to the Ishmaelites, and let not our hand be upon him ; for he is our brother, our flesh."—*Old Test.*

Miscellaneous Examples.[1]

(*a*) *Convert the following from Direct to Indirect* :—

1. A stag, seeing his shadow in the water, said to himself, "What a pity it is that so fine a creature as I am should have so slender a set of legs ! What a grand animal I should be, if only my legs were as fine as my horns !"

2. The same stag, being afterwards hunted and held

[1] *To the Teacher.*—It is of course optional with the teacher to have the examples given under (*a*) and (*b*) shown up to him in written form, if he considers that the students will not be able to read an example off at sight after having first read it aloud *slowly* to the class. We advise, however, that the students be allowed a trial ; for, though some of the examples look rather formidable from their length, they are much easier than they look, and we believe that by perseverance and practice, and with perhaps some assistance at first from the teacher, every student, who has been well grounded in the previous chapters, will be able to read off these "Miscellaneous Examples" at sight, in spite of the length and apparent difficulty of some of them.

fast in a bush by his horns, said to himself, "How ill do we judge what is best for us! The legs which I despised would have borne me away in safety, if the horns of which I was so proud had not brought me to ruin."

3. "What do you mean?" asked the man; "how can a rope be used for binding flour?" "A rope can be used for anything," replied the man, "when I do not wish to lend it."

4. Once a rich man said to his poorer brother, "Why do you not enter the service of the king, so that you may relieve yourself from the baseness of labour?"

5. Finding no remedy, Androcles said to himself, "It is better to die than to live in such misery as I am compelled to suffer from a master who treats me, and always has treated me, so cruelly."

6. They said one to another, "We are verily guilty concerning our brother, in that we saw the distress of his soul, when he besought us, and we would not hear; therefore is this distress come upon us."—*Old Test.*

7. "I am sorry indeed," replied the king, "that my vessel is already chosen, and that I cannot therefore sail with the son of the man who served my father."—DICKENS.

8. He cried to them in an agony, "Row back at any risk! I cannot bear to leave her behind to be drowned."—DICKENS.

9. "Which of these three men," said Jesus, "was neighbour unto him who fell among the robbers?" And he (the lawyer) said, "He that showed mercy on him." Jesus said unto him, "Go, and do thou likewise."—*New Test.*

10. "Since yesterday," he observed, "the wind has changed, and Damon will soon be here. Make haste, therefore," said he to the executioner, "and do your office."

11. The two combatants, seeing that a third person had carried off the prize they were fighting for, said to one another, "Ah! what fools we have been! We have been injuring one another only to fatten a rogue, who had no claim either way."

12. "Stop, stop," cried the two cats, who saw that each piece of cheese was rapidly going into the monkey's mouth, "we do not wish the case to go any further; let the case be closed, and we will go away."

The monkey with a grave face replied: "The case cannot now be closed; you have asked me to make your two shares equal, and I am doing my best to make them so."

When at last the two pieces had been made equal, the cats said: "The case can now certainly be closed. Give us back what is left of each share. We thank you for what you have done."

"Yes," said the monkey, "the case is closed; your two shares have been made equal. But the judge must have his fee for the time that he has spent in hearing and deciding this difficult dispute." Saying this, he devoured all that was left.

"It would have been better," said the cats to each other, "to have come to some agreement between ourselves, instead of going before a judge and losing all that we had."—*Fable of the Two Cats at Law.*

13. "See, my sons," said the old man, "the power of union. As long as the sticks were bound together in one bundle, you could not break them. Bind yourselves together, then, with brotherly love, and no one will be able to harm you. But if you are divided by discord, you will fall a prey to every one who seeks to injure one."
—*Fable of the Old Man and his Sons.*

(*b*) *Convert the following from Indirect to Direct:*—

1. A king who had paid a large sum in advance to strangers for the purchase of some horses, told his chief minister to prepare a list of all the fools in the kingdom. The minister told him that he had done so already, and had placed the king's name at the top of the list.

The king, being angry, asked him why he had done so. To which the minister replied that the fact of His Majesty's having given so much money to strangers without knowing where they lived, and of his having paid for horses before he had seen them, was a clear proof of folly.

The king then asked him what he would do, if the strangers brought the horses that he had paid for. The minister answered that he would in that case strike His Majesty's name off the top of the list of fools and put the strangers' names there in its place.

2. In the war (described in a fable) between birds and beasts, the bat, thinking one day that the beasts would win, impressed upon them that he was not a bird, and challenged them to find a bird that had two rows of teeth in its head as the bat had, and that gave milk to its young.

Another day, when the beasts seemed likely to lose, the bat went over to the birds and insisted that he was a bird. How, he asked, could he be a beast,—what beast in the world could fly like him,—what bird could fly better than he could?

3. A prince, having secretly visited a prison-yard and seen five prisoners with chains on their wrists going to work, asked them one after another what fault they had committed for which they were placed in prison.

The first said that he had done no wrong, but that the chief witness against him had told a lie, and the lie was believed by the magistrate.

The second said that the judge, who put him in prison, had a spite against him, and had not given him a just trial.

The third said that he had been found guilty through a mistake, and that the judge, being a dull man, had not understood the case.

The fourth said that he had been taken for another man: the man who was guilty escaped, while the man condemned was innocent.

These four all begged the prince to pardon them and to order the keeper of the jail to give them their liberty.

The prince turned to the fifth man and inquired whether he also declared that he was innocent and demanded to be released.

The fifth man told a different kind of tale: he admitted with sorrow that he had stolen a purse, and dared not ask for pardon; he owned that he was guilty and deserved the punishment which he was then suffering.

The prince, hearing this confession, said that a man who had been so dishonest was not fit to live with such honest men as those four, all of whom had declared that they had done no wrong; guilty and innocent men, he said, ought not to be compelled to live under the same roof.

Then turning to the jailor he told him to take that man's chains off and send him away, since he had not added to his faults, as the other four had done, the fault of telling a lie.

4. A trumpeter, having been overtaken on the battle field, begged that he might be spared. He pleaded that he had slain no man; that he carried nothing worse than a trumpet, which was merely a signal for battle; and that no one had ever yet been killed by a trumpet.

The soldiers told him in reply that they would slay him for the very reason that he was a trumpeter; for though he did not kill any men himself, he incited others to do so, and was therefore quite as mischievous as men who fought.

5. A fox, who had lost his tail, called the other foxes together, and standing with his back against a tree, told them that the tail was of no use and should be cut off; and that if all agreed to do this, no one could feel ashamed of having lost it.

The tail, he said, was the source of all their dangers; for the fox was hunted for the sake of its tail, and not for the sake of its flesh or fur.

An old fox thanked the speaker for his advice, but asked him to explain why he kept his back so firmly fixed against the stump of that tree; and begged him to turn himself round, and let them see what sort of a tail he had, and how he would look without one.—*Æsop's Fables.*

6. A lark, who had reared her young ones in a field of corn that was nearly ripe enough to be harvested, instructed them to take particular notice of what the owner of the field might say in her absence, whenever she might be forced to go away in search of food.

On the first day, when the owner entered the field, they heard him say to his son that the corn seemed ripe enough to be cut, and that he (the son) must go early next day and request their friends, who dwelt in four or five houses near at hand, to come and help them to cut it.

The mother, having learnt from her young ones what the master had said, bade them not to be afraid; for she was sure (she said) that if the master of the field depended on his friends and neighbours, the corn would not be cut on the morrow.

Next day the master came to the field with his son; but finding no neighbours there to help him, he told his son to run off that instant to his uncle and request him to come on the morrow with his three sons and give a helping hand to the reaping of the corn; for it was evident that those friends and neighbours on whom he had depended were not to be trusted.

The mother, on hearing all this from her young ones, told them not to be alarmed; for kinsmen were often no better than neighbours in helping one another; but she cautioned them to keep their ears open, and let her know what they might hear next.

On the third day the owner, on coming to the field and finding no one there to help him as before, told his son that, as neither neighbours nor kinsmen would give any assistance, it was quite evident they must do the reaping themselves; so he had better bring a couple of sickles, and with these they would set to work at once.

The lark on hearing this told her young ones that it was then time for them to go; for when a man resolved to do his work himself, it was not likely that the work would long remain undone.—*Fable of the Lark and her Young Ones.*

CHAPTER VI.—ORDER OF WORDS AND PHRASES.

67. Importance of Order.—If words and phrases are not put in their right places, the sense of a sentence is either rendered doubtful or destroyed altogether. Observe how the sense of the following sentences is marred by the faulty order of some of the words:—

(1) A piano is offered for sale by a lady about to cross the Channel in an oak case with carved legs.

(2) He blew out his brains after bidding his wife good-bye with a gun.

(3) Erected to the memory of John Phillips accidentally shot as a mark of affection by his brother.

(4) The University of London Commissioners.—*Daily Telegraph*, Aug. 6, 1898.

(5) The above is a reproduction of the magnificent picture by the celebrated French artist Benjamin Constant, representing the interior of a carpet bazaar in Tanjiers, now in the possession of Messrs. Treloar and Sons, Ludgate Hill.—*Black and White*, p. 191, Aug. 6, 1898.

(6) *Paradise Lost* is the name of Milton's great epic poem on the loss of Paradise divided into twelve separate parts.

(7) You have already been informed of the sale of Ford's theatre where Mr. Lincoln was assassinated for religious purposes.

(8) Few people learn anything that is worth learning easily.

(9) He was shot by a secretary under notice to quit with whom he was finding fault very fortunately without effect.

(10) He repeated these lines after he had read them only once with perfect accuracy.

(11) Our correspondent saw several soldiers dead or wounded riding over the battlefield.

68. Cardinal rule about Order.—The cardinal rule about order is this:—*Things that are to be thought of together must be mentioned together.* In every one of the above examples this rule has been violated. For instance, in the first example we have *in an oak case* joined to "about to cross the Channel" instead of being joined to "piano."

By attending to the rule above given, we can correct the above sentences as follows:—

(1) A piano in an oak case with carved legs is offered for sale by a lady about to cross the Channel.

(2) After bidding his wife good-bye, he blew out his brains with a gun.

(3) Erected by his brother as a mark of affection, to the memory of John Phillips, accidentally shot.

(4) The Commissioners of London University; or, The London University Commissioners.

(5) The above, now in the possession of Messrs. Treloar and Sons, Ludgate Hill, is a reproduction of the magnificent picture, representing the interior of a carpet bazaar in Tanjiers, by the celebrated French artist, Benjamin Constant.

(6) *Paradise Lost*, divided into twelve separate parts, is the name of Milton's great epic poem on the loss of Paradise.

(7) You have already been informed of the sale, for religious purposes, of Ford's theatre, where Mr. Lincoln was assassinated.

(8) Few people learn easily anything that is worth learning.

(9) He was shot, fortunately without effect, by a secretary under notice to quit, with whom he was finding fault.

(10) After he had read these lines only once, he repeated them with perfect accuracy.

(11) Riding over the battlefield, our correspondent saw several soldiers dead or wounded.

69. Verb and Subject.—As a general rule the Subject is placed before its verb. But if the verb is Intransitive, and the Subject is accompanied by a good deal of description, it is convenient to place the subject after the verb:—

During the supremacy of Northumbria lived *the Venerable Bede*, who wrote a history of the English

Church, which is the earliest history of our race written by an Englishman.—*Short Hist. Eng.*, p. 18.

Before you spreads *an expanse* of English lawn, only broken by clumps of gay-foliaged shrubs or beds of flowers.—*Rev. of Reviews*, p. 369, April 1900.

The verbs of these sentences would sound very bald, if the Subjects were placed before them instead of after them:—

During the supremacy of Northumbria, the Venerable Bede, who wrote a history of the English Church, which is the earliest history of our race written by an Englishman, lived.

Before you an expanse of English lawn, only broken by clumps of gay-foliaged shrubs or beds of flowers, spreads.

Observe, however, that when a verb is thus placed before its Subject, it must not be made the first word of the sentence. It should be introduced by some phrase, such as "During the supremacy of Northumbria," or "Before you" (see the two examples given), or at least by some short adverb; as "Thus," "There," "Then," etc.:—

Then fell the kingdom of the Goths.—SOUTHEY.
Down went the Royal George.—COWPER.

Note.—The general rule given above, that the Subject is placed before its verb, and not after it, applies only to Assertive sentences; that is, sentences which state some fact, real or supposed. If the sentence asks a question or expresses a wish, the Subject is always after the verb:—

When will *he* come? Long live *the king!*

70. Verb and Object.—As a general rule the Object is placed immediately after its verb, and nothing is allowed to come between them. Sometimes, however, it is convenient to separate them by an adverb, or even by a long adverbial phrase, when the said adverb or phrase is used to qualify the verb :—

> The captain took *with a cheerful heart* the good things which the firm provided.

Observe, that if the adverbial phrase italicised had not been placed where it is, the sense would have been radically altered :—

> The captain took the good things which the firm provided with a cheerful heart.

Such a lengthy insertion as the following is admissible, when we see that the sense of the sentence requires it :—

> Jack meantime, who had just come below from his watch on deck, was attacking, *with a ferocity which made it appear as if he was contending with some bitter enemy instead of a plentiful dinner*, the boiled beef and biscuit that the boy had lately placed on the table.—KINGSTON, *Three Midshipmen*, ch. ii.

Observe how extremely awkward the above sentence would be if the order of words were changed :—

> Jack meantime, who had just come below from his watch on deck, was attacking the boiled beef and biscuit that the boy had lately placed on the table with a ferocity which made it appear as if he was contending with some bitter enemy instead of a plentiful dinner.

71. Noun with Adjective or Participle.—As a general rule an adjective or participle, or other qualifying word that does the work of an adjective, is placed immediately before the noun that it qualifies; and it is very important to bear this rule in mind. Thus there is a great difference between—

> The author's best endeavours—The best author's endeavours.

A great gentleman's coat—A gentleman's greatcoat.

A little lady's dog—A lady's little dog.

An unquestioned man of genius—A man of unquestioned genius.

The half-yearly Directors' meeting—The Directors' half-yearly meeting.

Nevertheless it is convenient to place the adjective or participle after the noun, if it is enlarged by some qualifying phrase or clause:—

A matter too *urgent to be put off any longer.*

A room not *large enough for a meeting that was likely to be attended by twenty persons.*

A man *convinced against his will* is of the same opinion still.

If the participle is one formed with the help of an Auxiliary verb, it may stand either before or after the noun:—

The horse, *being tired out*, could go no further.
Being tired out, the horse could go no further.

When several adjectives qualify the same noun, it often sounds better to place the noun first:—

God is the maker of all things *visible and invisible, animate and inanimate.*

The Lords *spiritual and temporal.*

There are a few well-established phrases, in which the adjective is placed last:—

Notary *public.* Heir *apparent.* Governor-*general.* The sum *total.* Letters *patent.* Knight-*errant.*

When the adjectives connected with a noun express entirely different meanings, it may be advantageous to separate them by placing the noun in the middle:—

One of the most extraordinary things is *the utter past and present neglect* of British interests in Somaliland.—*Daily Tel.*, p. 10, May 7, 1901. (The sense will be more obvious, and the sound will be more pleasing, if we say "The utter neglect, past and present, of British interests," etc.)

72. Verb with Adjective or Participle.—When the sense of an adjective or participle is more closely connected with that of the verb of the sentence than with that of the Subject or Object, the adjective or participle must be placed both after the noun and after the verb. An adjective or participle so used can be called Complementary, because it completes the sense of the verb.

(*a*) *Subject*:—

He became *sad* and *dispirited*.
He was found *carrying* his coat on his arm.

Here the italicised adjectives and participles, though they qualify the Subject *he*, are more closely connected in sense with the verb than with the subject.

(*b*) *Object*:—

They painted the door *white*.
They considered the man *courageous*.

Here *white*, though it qualifies the Object *door*, is still more closely connected in sense with the verb *painted*. Similarly *courageous* is closely connected in sense with the verb *considered*. Both adjectives are therefore placed after the noun as well as after the verb.

Observe how the sense of the following sentences depends on the position of the italicised adjectives:—

My father left *poor* me. (My father deserted unlucky me.)
My father left me *poor*. (When my father died, I had not much to support me.)

He bought *cheap* material. (He bought cheap material, paying for it at the market rate, whatever its quality may have been.)
He bought the material *cheap*. (He bought the material at a price below the market rate.)

{ I *alone* can do it. (No one but me can do it.)
{ I can do it *alone*. (I can do it without any assistance.)

73. Relative and Antecedent.—A Relative pronoun or Relative adverb should be placed as close as possible to its antecedent :—

(1) I have read Plato's writings, who was a disciple of Socrates.

Say, "I have read the writings of Plato, who was a disciple of Socrates."

(2) It is the system, not the individual, which I condemn.

Say, "It is the system which I condemn, not the individual"; or, "It is not the individual, but the system which I condemn."

(3) I now come to one of the objections to free trade, which has never yet been answered.

Say, "Among the objections to free trade, I now come to one which has never yet been answered."

74. Noun and Demonstrative pronoun. — A Demonstrative pronoun, being a word of reference, should not as a rule be mentioned until the word to which it refers has been mentioned. This rule is neglected in the following sentence :—

Before we pay *them*, let us see what work *the men* have done. (Say, "Before we pay *the men*, let us see what work *they* have done.")

75. Adverb. — The positions of an adverb are various.

(*a*) *With Adjective, Preposition, Conjunction, or other Adverb.*—Let the adverb or adverbial phrase be placed immediately before any of the parts of speech just named :—

Adj. or Part.	We are *half* pleased and *half* sorry. He seems to be *a good deal* annoyed.
Preposition.	By that time he was *half* across the river. He came *three hours* before the time.
Conjunction.	He spoke as he did *only* because he was angry. He came *three hours* before the door was opened.
Other Adverb.	This news reached us *very* lately. *Four days* later other news was received.

(*b*) *With Intransitive verb.*—When the verb is Intransitive, the adverb is generally placed after the verb, not before. But if the Adverb denotes time, it is generally placed before the verb:—

He *always* laughed *heartily* at a good joke.
He *never* spoke *boastfully* about his own merits.

The tendency to place adverbs of time first is so strong in our language, that we sometimes find such an adverb placed before the wrong word:—

His last journey was to Cannes, whence he was never destined to return.—MRS. GROTE, *Life of George Grote*, ch. xxix. p. 245. (Say "Destined never to return.")

Note.—If the tense of the verb (whether Transitive or Intransitive) is formed with an Auxiliary verb, an adverb or adverbial phrase can be placed between the Auxiliary and the Principal verb:—

He *has always* laughed heartily at a good joke.
He *was much* pleased with his son's progress.
The colonist had *for an insignificant sum* purchased a valuable estate, which was only ten miles away from Sydney.

(*c*) *With Transitive verb.*—When the verb is Transitive, the adverb can be placed either before the verb or after the Object:—

He bore his loses *cheerfully.*
He *briefly* explained his meaning.

If the Object is accompanied by many other words, the adverb can be placed between the verb and the Object:—

He liberally rewarded—or He rewarded liberally—all those who had assisted him.

It adds much to the energy and sometimes to the perspicuity of a sentence, if the adverb **only** is placed immediately before the word which it is intended to qualify:—

Sir George added that England would remain a world-power *only so long as* it held command of the sea.—*Daily Express*, p. 5, Sept. 7, 1900. (This is much better than saying "would only remain.")

Russia is willing to act in concert with the other powers *only until* order has been restored in China, and no longer.—*Daily Telegraph*, p. 9, July 7, 1900. (This is much better than saying "is only willing," etc.)

He looked forward to a time when all our main cables would *only touch* British territory, and would be adequately protected from an enemy.—*Ibid.*, p. 6, Sept. 7, 1900. (Here the order is so bad that it alters the sense. It should be "would touch only British territory.")

(*d*) Whenever an adverb or adverbial phrase qualifies a whole sentence rather than any particular word, it stands the first word in the sentence. Observe how the sense of the following sentences depends on the position of the adverb:—

Happily he did not die. (It is a happy result that he did not die.)
He did not die *happily*. (He did not die in a happy state of mind.)

At length he wrote to her. (At last, after a good deal of delay, he wrote to her.)
He wrote to her *at length.* (He wrote her a long letter.)

76. Order of Prepositions.—Whenever a preposition is used, there must be two words that go with it: one is the dependent word (*i.e.* the word dependent on the preposition), which is called its Object; the other is the principal word, on which the preposition itself depends. "A bird in the hand": here *hand* is the object or dependent word, and *bird* is the principal word.

The Object of a preposition is always a noun or noun-equivalent. The principal word may be either a noun, or an adjective, or an adverb, or a verb:—

(a)	*Noun.*	A *bird* in the hand.	A *box* of tools.
	Adjective.	*Slothful* in business.	*Short* of money.
	Adverb.	*Independently* of me.	*Adversely* to my interests.
(b)	*Verb.*	He *sat* on the grass.	He *did* everything in a hurry.

(*a*) If the principal word is a noun, or an adjective, or an adverb, the preposition with its Object is placed immediately after it, or if not immediately after, as close after it as possible. This rule is broken in the following examples:—

One of the combatants was unhurt, and the other sustained a wound in the arm of no importance. Quoted in *Punch*, Oct. 5, 1872. (Say, "sustained in the arm a wound of no importance.")

One longed to copy the picture with jewels, as some skilful Mosaicist had copied Da Vinci's "Last Supper" in Vienna.—MISS EDWARDS, *A Winter with the Swallows*, ch. ii. p. 20. (Say, "some skilful Mosaicist in Vienna.")

Such a camp would afford an opportunity for giving a different kind of instruction and training, but one no less valuable perhaps, from that which is given in the schoolroom.—*Rev. of Reviews*, p. 611, Dec. 1899. (The sentence can be recast as follows: "Such a camp would afford an opportunity of giving instruction and training of a kind different from, but perhaps not less valuable than, that," etc.)

When the principal word has more than one preposition depending on it, it is sometimes convenient to put one of the prepositions with its Object first:—

Herod is bound, body and soul, by an overwhelming passion to his haughty and beautiful wife.—*Fort. Review*, p. 180, Jan. 1901.

The proximity of *passion* alongside of *to* is awkward. If we retain the order of the words in the above sentence, we might change *passion to* to *passion for*. But we can get over the difficulty by altering the order and saying:

By an overwhelming passion Herod is bound, body and soul, to his haughty and beautiful wife.

(*b*) If the principal word is a verb, the preposition with its Object may be placed either before or after it; but it must in either case be placed near enough to prevent ambiguity or an unpleasing effect. This rule is violated in such examples as the following:—

In 1238 Henry gave him his sister Eleanor, widow of the eldest son of William Marshall, the Regent, in marriage.—*Short Hist. Eng.*, p. 100. (Say, "gave him in marriage.")

It was with the approval of Mr. Balfour and Mr. Chamberlain that the Secretary of the Local Government Board withdrew the schedule fixing a maximum rate of interest from the Money-lending Bill. — *Daily Telegraph*, p. 9, June 28, 1900. (Say, "withdrew from the Money-lending Bill.")

One could not help coveting the privileges they enjoyed for one's sister.—MISS EDWARDS, *A Winter with the Swallows*, ch. xiv. p. 236. (Say "coveting for one's sister.")

77. Conjunctions that go in pairs.—Correlative conjunctions (*i.e.* conjunctions that go in pairs), such as *not . . . but, not only . . . but also, not more . . . than, both . . . and, either . . . or, neither . . . nor*, should be made to occupy corresponding positions, *i.e.* each member of the pair should be placed before words of the same or a similar part of speech. Observe the violation of this rule in the following examples:—

The Greek language had obtained such a vogue in Rome itself, that all the great and noble men of the city were obliged not only to learn, but ambitious everywhere to speak it.—MIDDLETON, *Life of Cicero*, vol. i. p. 94. (Say, "were not only obliged to learn, but ambitious everywhere," etc. The participle *obliged* is of a similar part of speech to the adjective *ambitious*.")

He was neither fitted by abilities nor disposition to answer the wishes of his mother and sister.—MISS AUSTEN, *Sense and Sensibility*, vol. i. p. 31. (Say, "neither by abilities nor by disposition.")

In the Democratic platform, therefore, we find trusts not only severely denounced, but a remedy for the evil suggested. — *Review of Reviews*, p. 356, Oct. 1900. (Say, "we find not only," etc.)

78. "As well as," "no less than," "no more than."—Care must be taken to place these conjunctional phrases between the words that they are intended to combine. Observe how the sense of the following sentences depends on the order of the words:—

> The troopers needed food as well as horses.
> The troopers as well as the horses needed food.

Exercises on Chapter VI. (To be done orally and at sight.)

Rearrange or recast the following sentences in such a way as to correct or remove any fault that may exist in the order of the words:—

I. Examples chiefly coined.

1. The chair cost ten shillings on which he sat.
2. He shot the mad dog after driving it out of the house with a gun.
3. He is an undoubted man of honesty, and yet persons accused him of cheating who ought to have known better.
4. This tablet was erected to the memory of a faithful dog that was accidentally shot as a mark of respect.
5. He left the house where he had slept next morning mounted on a horse.
6. He repeated those lines after he had read them only once with perfect accuracy.
7. The judge saw more clearly that the man was innocent than the jury did.
8. The girl was conveyed from the house where she had just been married in a carriage and pair.
9. They found the house on the top of a hill where they wished to spend the night.
10. It is believed that they are most desirous of keeping up this custom who profit most by it.
11. There was a small house on the side of the mountain, out of which came a black slave.
12. The magistrate passed too severe a sentence on the accused, being young and inexperienced.
13. English is not only difficult to speak, but also to spell.

14. The general ordered the deserters to be shot indignantly.

15. I only like a pear when it is ripe.

16. A gang of robbers entered the house at night armed from head to foot.

17. Northern India is bounded by the Himalaya mountains, with at their base a very thick jungle.

18. The inhabitants of the other islands only know how to divide time by the sun and moon, whereas these islanders had acquired some knowledge of the stars also.

19. I soon arrived at the mansion of my friend, guarded by a huge mastiff that flew at me.

20. Sir Martin Peto spoke of the notion that the National Debt might be repudiated with absolute contempt.

21. I am neither an ascetic in theory nor practice.

22. I never remember to have felt an event more deeply than Horner's death.

23. Her success is neither the result of system nor strategy.

24. His last journey was to Cannes, whence he was never destined to return.

25. His daily custom is to tell anecdotes which amuse or excite the company after dinner.

26. Some paintings by lady artists, well worthy of inspection, will be exhibited to-morrow.

27. The daughter of a civil officer retired from India, brought up in England, seeks employment.

28. Lost a walking-stick belonging to a gentleman with a curiously shaped head.

29. Here the train made a halt to take in water, which lasted only a few minutes.

30. Do you take the medicine that I send you regularly?

31. I never remember to have spent a more agreeable visit.

32. His body was found floating lifeless on the water at a short distance from where the boat was upset by a fisherman.

33. Milton left several poems of which he had written the outlines in an unfinished state.

34. Wanted a rocking-horse for a small child with a long mane and tail.

35. After the papers have been given out it is requested that no candidate will enter or leave the examination-hall except by the side door.

36. He contributed several essays to the leading periodicals which are marked by much research and great originality of method.

37. It is not necessary to define a technical term that is used in a scientific treatise more than once.

38. Zedekiah was sent captive to Babylon, from which he was never destined to return.

39. I saw that the prisoner at the bar was guilty with half an eye.

40. I was very anxious to tell him to leave the room without giving offence.

41. He carried out the contract which he had undertaken honestly and punctually.

II. Examples all genuine.

1. He cannot be said to have died prematurely whose work was finished, nor does he deserve to be lamented who died so full of honours.—SOUTHEY.

2. Since several thoughts may be natural which are low and grovelling, an epic poet should not only avoid such sentiments as are unnatural or affected, but also such as are mean and vulgar.—ADDISON, *Spectator*, No. 279.

3. This shipping is to a great extent now the product of German yards, which have developed rapidly to suit the requirements every day increasing of local shipbuilding.—*Daily Telegraph*, January 27, 1898.

4. There are not meanwhile critics wanting here, who assign this victory as regards moral and political supremacy in China to Russia.—Berlin Telegram, *Daily Telegraph*, Feb. 5, 1898.

5. The sitting closed definitely at five o'clock without the matter which had brought so many together having

been practically entered upon.—*Daily Tel.*, February 8, 1898.

6. The death occurred last week in Madrid of Mr. W. Macpherson, formerly British Vice-Consul at Seville.—*Times Weekly*, February 11, 1898.

7. No one is entitled to form or express an opinion on the relations between Nelson and Lady Hamilton, or on the parentage of Horatia, who has not carefully studied the letters to be found in this invaluable collection.—*Times Weekly*, March 4, 1898.

8. It will be a war on sea instead of land largely, and we do not know much about sea warfare of late years.—Quoted in *Daily Tel.*, April 15, 1898.

9. From the very day of the birth of a Spanish monarch he is subject to an etiquette the most pronounced.—*Cassell's Family Magazine*, p. 149, January 1897.

10. We may well ask what is the use of it, if energetic action in shipbuilding is not accompanied by parallel action in diplomacy.—*Homeward Mail*, July 25, 1898.

11. Remains only the Great Western Railway Company, and some five score of Ealing residents, who have yielded to the solicitations of an agent of the London General Omnibus Company.—*Middlesex Co. Times*, p. 5, April 28, 1900.

12. These excellent villas to be sold or let, freehold or leasehold.—*Builder's Notice.*

13. He was a saint indeed, not a hermit of asceticism, combining piety, meekness, humility, simplicity, with active benevolence and virtue.—GOLDWIN SMITH, *United Kingdom*, vol. i. p. 48.

14. Articles appear in our page for women dealing with "Early Autumn Fashions," "The Ladies' Golf Union," and "Russian Society."—*Daily Tel.*, p. 8, Sept. 9, 1899.

15. I shall not trouble you further, disliking controversy.—Quoted in *Spectator*, p. 747, Nov. 24, 1900.

16. For Herodias' sake, his brother Philip's wife.—*Matth.* xiv. 3.

17. If he is still alive, it may be found possible to

establish the Emperor on the throne.—*Daily Express*, p. 4, June 20, 1900.

18. An exhibition has just been closed at Manchester, which should be interesting to many more persons than those of the trade.—*Daily Graphic*, p. 7, May 26, 1900.

19. I am not minded to follow in Rufinus's tracks, whose story I was about to tell thee.—*Quo Vadis*, ch. i. p. 28.

20. They tell him that there shall be no reforms in the slovenly methods common enough fifty years ago, some of which have survived to the present day, of which he does not approve.—*Church Gazette*, p. 710, April 15, 1899.

21. I never made the statement at the last meeting of the County Council or at any other time, which you have imputed to me.—*Middlesex Co. Times*, p. 9, June 9, 1900.

22. The allies will only be able to test the reality of the apparent awakening of the fighting spirit in China, when they are in a position to carry on the operations upon ground permitting the evolution of flanking tactics. —*Daily Tel.*, p. 9, July 18, 1900.

23. It leads the reader who seeks to understand the real bent of Ruskin's sympathy astray.—Quoted in *Rev. of Reviews*, p. 247, March 1900.

24. He had already made strong representations to the imperial Government to refrain from sending the prisoners to St. Helena without success.—*Daily Tel.*, p. 7, March 30, 1900.

25. At Paris I only found a different view in regard to the South African war in the house of a well-known Parliamentarian and honorary member of the Cobden Club.—*Fortnightly Review*, p. 33, July 1900.

26. There is a huge cave among its cliffs, where the Mac Somethings had taken refuge from their foes, the Mac Something Elses, to the number of above two hundred men.—*Church Gazette*, p. 41, April 29, 1899.

27. Lessons are only attended to there in the morning. —*Literature*, p. 262, March 31, 1900.

28. A month ago it is reported that M. Delcassé was only restrained at the eleventh hour by the intervention

of the Premier from formally raising the question of the date of our retirement from Egypt.—*Rev. of Reviews*, p. 312, April 1900.

29. Lord Palmerston refused to join Lord Derby on a fraudulent pretext.—*The Press*, Feb. 1885.

30. People ceased to wonder by degrees. — MRS. OLIPHANT, *Chronicles of Carlingford*, ch. vi. p. 75.

31. He (Domitian) did not fail to persecute Christians because he had no inclination to do so, but because there were none in Rome during his reign to persecute.—REBER, *Christ of Paul*, p. 241.

32. There is a sort of suspicion among quiet Germans, especially in the non-industrial provinces, that he wishes to pose as a redresser of the world's wrongs,—a suspicion which we entirely believe to be unjust.—*Spectator*, p. 737, Nov. 24, 1900.

33. It is also to be borne in mind that the construction of a railway through at present waste lands could lead to great developments.—*Rev. of Reviews*, p. 580, Dec. 1899.

34. In a recent number of *Literature* the discovery at Florence was announced of a series of documents bearing on the family of Dante.—*Literature*, p. 319, Sept. 30, 1899.

35. At Trefriw in Wales is to be seen a danger-board which states: "Notice to Cyclists—This hill is dangerous by order of the authorities." While they were in the vein, they might as well have ordered it to be safe.—*Daily Tel.*, p. 7, Aug. 26, 1899.

36. Lord Stanhope will call attention to the effect on the operation of the Sugar bounties of recent legislation in India.—*Ibid.*, p. 7, July 20, 1899.

37. Subtle, proud, daring, resolute, and an accomplished hypocrite, she disguises a long-cherished hatred of her husband, resulting from the sacrifice of her daughter at Aulis, under the cloak of a love-sick affection.—PALEY'S *Æschylus*, p. 320.

38. The restriction sometimes whets the desire for a change into fierceness.—JONES, *Holiday Papers*, p. 20.

39. In theory every knot of increased speed above twenty knots gives an approximate reduction in the time

of the voyage of seven hours.—*Daily Tel.*, p. 8, Dec. 26, 1899.

40. The Dutch government is resolved to set its face against any demonstrations, nor will it permit Mr. K. to establish a centre of political intrigue against a friendly Power in Holland.—*Ibid.*, p. 9, Oct. 25, 1900.

41. According to the same correspondent, the British Consul at Marseilles has made an investigation, together with a police-official, as to the incident which took place yesterday.—*Ibid.*, p. 9, Nov. 24, 1900.

42. It has too often been our habit in dealing with the Chinese to forget the crimes committed by them on the first appearance of repentance.—*Blackwood's Magazine*, p. 289, Aug. 1900.

43. The writer contemplates the possibility of the conversion of the four hundred millions of China into a military people with dread.—*Rev. of Reviews*, p. 290, March 1901.

44. There has just died at Clapham a gentlewoman whose demise will not only be regretted by all those who knew her, but by every constable throughout the metropolis.—*Daily Tel.*, p. 10, Oct. 18, 1900.

45. When this prevails in Madras schools, the centre of education, worse will be the case of village schools.—*Educ. Review* (Madras), p. 63, Feb. 1900.

46. As the leading and consistent champion of the oppressed, I trust you will permit me in your columns to advocate the cause of humanity towards helpless animals. —Quoted in *Daily Tel.*, Jan. 6, 1898.

47. Behind them stood great Berlin houses, and behind these was another imperial policy than the policy of imperial England.—Quoted in *Rev. of Reviews*, p. 156, Feb. 15, 1899.

48. Political bitterness only yields the palm to religious.—*Educ. Rev.* (Madras), p. 59, Feb. 1900.

49. He seldom took up the Bible, which he frequently did, without shedding tears.—KNOWLES, *Life of Fuseli*, vol. i. p. 389.

50. The cordon has been drawn, which is, if possible,

to prevent the raiders now retiring before the great British force which is working through the eastern portions of the colony from the north from breaking away southwards.—*Daily Tel.*, p. 10, Oct. 11, 1900.

51. There remains a very copious supply of creditable literature in the autumn lists to be dealt with.—*Fort. Rev.*, p. 1028, Dec. 1900.

52. What were, so to speak, the ground-plan of that marvellous character, the inherent qualities that composed the man, I may be allowed to quote from a work of my own.—*Ibid.*, p. 132, Jan. 1901.

CHAPTER VII.—THE USE AND DISCRIMINATION OF WORDS.[1]

SECTION 1.—TO SUBSTITUTE EQUIVALENT WORDS.

79. Equivalent Words.—In the following exercises the student is required to substitute for each word printed in italics some other word, the use of which will make no appreciable difference in the sense of the sentence. The words exchanged need not be exact equivalents. For instance, in describing an east wind, it comes to the same thing whether we call it *biting* or *cutting*. In other contexts "to bite" is not the same thing as "to cut"; yet the two words *biting*

[1] *To the Teacher.*—The object of the present chapter is to help the student to acquire a ready command, combined with a right use, of words—especially such words as he is likely to have picked up from what he hears spoken around him and from what he may have seen in books and newspapers. To teach promptness, and at the same time to excite attention, we advise that all the exercises be done orally in class and without previous preparation. The student should be told to read the sentence slowly aloud to the class, and then to read it out a second time with a new word substituted for the one printed in italics. To prevent a student from looking ahead to the sentence which will come to his turn, either the order of sentences as given in the book should not be adhered to, or the students should not be put on to read in their regular order in the class.

and *cutting*, when applied to a wind, convey the same impression to the mind of the hearer or reader, and one can be exchanged for the other without altering the sense. In the English language it is as difficult to find any two words that will mean exactly the same thing in all possible connections, as it would be in the natural world to find any two leaves precisely similar in colour, shape, and size. Yet it is possible to substitute one leaf for another in a nosegay without making any noticeable change in the general effect. The student is now asked to use a similar freedom in substituting one word for another, and to use it with equal skill and judgment, *i.e.* to use it in such a way as not to alter the sense of any sentence.

Exercises on § 79. (To be done orally and at sight.)

(*a*) *Substitute another verb for the italicised verb in each of the following, taking care that the sense of the sentence remains unaltered*:—

1. He was much *esteemed* by all who knew him.
2. One star *exceeds* another star in brightness.
3. The surplus profits were *divided* among the shareholders.
4. He deserves to be *commended* for his industry.
5. The law forbidding this practice has been *abrogated*.
6. I cannot even *conjecture* what his plans are.
7. The captain ordered his men to *halt*.
8. He never ceased to *bemoan* his losses.
9. At about ten o'clock the Orient *blew up* with a terrible shock.
10. That idea has long been *exploded*: no one now holds it.
11. We justly *rebuked* him for acting so selfishly.
12. I have no one to *help* me in this matter.
13. On hearing such a report he was much *surprised*.
14. That incident seriously *damaged* his reputation.

15. He completely *mastered* his difficulty by perseverance.

16. He was mean enough to *forsake* his friend in trouble.

17. I *confide* in your honesty and *accept* what you say.

18. We have *resided* four years in this town.

19. He *tried* several times to jump over that fence, but failed.

20. I was a good deal *annoyed* at being so *distrusted.*

21. He *asserted* his right to be heard in his defence.

22. I could not *ascertain* what had really *happened.*

23. I do not *anticipate* that any good will come of it.

24. His judgment was *warped* by prejudice.

25. *Strive* to *conquer* your weakness, and *conquer* it you will.

26. He took the wrong road, because he was *misled.*

27. We must *give up* all hope of coming here again.

28. One who knows that he is *suspected* feels *discouraged.*

29. It would be rash to *rely* on that man's promises.

30. He was a good deal *disturbed* by all those worries.

31. The Saxon army was *routed* at the Battle of Hastings.

32. I *foresee* much difficulty in carrying out that project.

33. The terms offered by the enemy were *rejected.*

34. It was a work of great labour to *scale* that hill.

35. I have been *asked* to write a report on that matter.

36. The offence was not intentional, but we *craved* his pardon.

37. The petition was *backed* by two hundred signatures.

38. My plans have been *frustrated* by his opposition.

39. The boat was *capsized* by the suddenness of the gale.

40. He was not *permitted* to say such things again.

41. He *hastened* along as fast as his horse could carry him.

42. This is not the pattern that I should have *selected.*

43. Our journey was *finished* by about 4 P.M.

44. He *lingered* on the road much more than he need have done.

45. My feelings have been *wounded* by that remark.
46. A large new house will be *erected* on that site.
47. This river will *impede* our progress.
48. The city was *encompassed* by the enemy.
49. Such a foolish custom as that will not *last* long.
50. Why was the name of that student *left out?*
51. His progress was *arrested* by an unlucky accident.
52. The man who had the stolen watch was *apprehended.*
53. The man is innocent and should be *liberated.*
54. The horse stepped out as soon as the driver *loosened* the reins.
55. I do not *understand* what you are driving at.
56. He *acquired* much wealth in the practice of his profession.
57. His mind needs to be *directed* in the right path.
58. I do not *consider* that you have *acted* wisely.
59. It is a pity that he cannot *govern* his temper.
60. In this hot season the cattle are *teased* by the flies.
61. The booty was *distributed* amongst the soldiers.
62. I *question* his right to close that gate against the public.
63. The fine that he had to pay *came* to ten pounds.
64. The workmen *collected* near the pay office.
65. The dispute was not *decided* by the evening.
66. *Fasten* these sticks together into a fagot.
67. The old man *called* his sons around him.
68. I cannot *calculate* what this change will cost me.
69. I have *purchased* a yoke of oxen.
70. Every one will *observe* what you are doing.
71. It is of no use to *dispute* about differences of taste.
72. Which of us can *force* that man to hold his tongue.
73. You have always been *looked upon* as the cleverer.
74. The hare *retreated* behind a bush.
75. The men have decided to *strike* work.
76. He would not *agree* to give them higher wages.
77. They were *tired out* with the heat, and could hardly *move* along.
78. He has *given up* making any further attempt.

79. They are eager to *extend* their sphere of influence.
80. This point was *insisted on* long ago.
81. I *misinterpreted* his character.
82. A blind man cannot *discriminate* colours.
83. He *scrutinised* the accounts to some purpose.
84. We have often *admonished* him on that point.
85. I shall be more *obliged* to you than I can express.
86. The plan will not *answer;* try another.
87. That wall is *mantled* with ivy and other creepers.
88. The river has *inundated* the neighbouring fields.
89. The stars *sparkle* more brightly in a frosty night.
90. The waterfall *leaps* over the rocks.
91. He *hurried* along as fast as he could.
92. The river *meanders* slowly through the forest.
93. The mud of the river *enriches* the soil.
94. His meanness was severely *censured* by all.
95. Not one of his friends either *helped* or *encouraged* him.
96. The bone was *fractured* a little above the joint.
97. He *closed* his career as prosperously as he began it.
98. Did you *witness* the deed, or only hear of it?
99. The case must be *heard* again in another court.
100. They *challenged* him to do his worst.
101. The plan must be *relinquished* forthwith.
102. They *surrendered* after a short resistance.
103. His influence has been much *lessened* of late.
104. His influence has decidedly *fallen off.*
105. Such excuses are *contemned* by every one.
106. He was *coerced* into accepting these hard terms.
107. You cannot *force* a man to change his mind all at once.
108. The flower *faded* sooner than I expected.
109. The work was *carried out* to my satisfaction.
110. He *entreated* them to *give* him one more chance.
111. Nothing was done to *alleviate* the distress.
112. Your request is one that cannot be *complied with.*
113. No one *condoled* with him in his sorrow.
114. He felt *invigorated* by the change of air.
115. Nothing would make him *let out* the secret.

116. He is soon *irritated* and soon *appeased*.
117. He *continued* talking for another half-hour.
118. These efforts must be *renewed* day after day.
119. He *bequeathed* a large sum to a London hospital.
120. I do not *recollect* half of what he told me.
121. I do not *see* what your motives could have been.
122. Let nothing be done to *retard* his progress.
123. Geography is a mind-*expanding* subject.
124. The surface of the water was *ruffled* by the breeze.
125. You had better *accelerate* your pace, or you will be late.
126. The trains *collided*, coming from opposite directions.
127. The boat-race was *put off* for another week.
128. Such a result could not have been *foreseen*.
129. They *dawdled* a long time on the road.
130. I am fond of *roaming* about in the fields.
131. The ship is *propelled* partly by sail and partly by steam.
132. One's mind *recoils* from such a dreadful thought.
133. He was *exiled* from his country for that crime.
134. The lambs are *gamboling* in the fields.
135. I cannot *help* his being angry with me.
136. It is better not to *meddle* with other people.
137. The two companies *combined* for their mutual advantage.
138. The pleasure of the visit was *marred* by his illness.
139. We *besought* him to take more care of himself.
140. He *prevailed on* us to grant his request.
141. An ink-spot is not easily *erased*.
142. A.'s courage cannot be *matched* with B.'s.
143. The crops will fail, unless the fields are *irrigated*.
144. It was found necessary to *amputate* the leg.
145. I *contemplate* making a few more changes.
146. While no one was looking, the money *vanished*.
147. Your view of the matter does not *tally* with mine.

(*b*) *Substitute another noun for the italicised noun in each of the following, taking care that the sense of the sentence remains unaltered :—*

1. I cannot place much *reliance* on his promise.
2. The *invalid* is better to-day than he was yesterday.
3. He got fresh advice by calling in another *physician.*
4. The *complaint* from which he suffered gave us less anxiety.
5. They are still good friends, though there has been a *difference.*
6. A student should treat his master with *respect.*
7. England was much harassed by the *irruptions* of Danes.
8. By a very ingenious *contrivance* the prisoner escaped.
9. He lodges in the third *storey* of that house.
10. He amused the company with an interesting *story.*
11. There is a very thick *mist* this morning.
12. I declined to accept any of his *presents.*
13. The *insurgents* were much *incensed* by his proceedings.
14. A flash of lightning disclosed the *situation* of the two fleets.
15. It was his daily *custom* to take early exercise.
16. He lived in a fine *house* and wore grand *apparel.*
17. A. was his *partner* in crime and quite as guilty.
18. This book was designed on a very good *plan.*
19. *Kindness* sometimes succeeds where *rigour* fails.
20. I hope no *mishap* has befallen him on the way.
21. I feel no *inclination* to do what he desires.
22. You have my full *permission* to take a day's change.
23. He shows no *tidiness* in his dress.
24. I have no *faith* in the *sincerity* of his professions.
25. No *improvement* can be made without *application* to work.
26. That *act* of his was a fine example of *bravery.*
27. The *conflict,* though long doubtful, ended in the *triumph* of the French.
28. Natural *loveliness* needs not the *aid* of fine *dress.*
29. She had a great *affection* for dumb animals.
30. I had a pleasant *talk* with him yesterday.
31. I am sorry to say I take no *delight* in music.
32. Without your *leave* he cannot leave the room.
33. He took much *trouble* to ascertain the facts.

34. His acquittal has filled me with *amazement.*
35. He has met with a serious *accident,* I fear.
36. There is no *enjoyment* in life without good health.
37. I have a great *dislike* to *solitude.*
38. He did me much *harm* by his bad advice.
39. Be careful to carry out the *directions* given you.
40. The *investment* of Ladysmith lasted several months.
41. A vast *stretch* of wild country lay in front of them.
42. He received a reward equal to his *merits.*
43. He showed a great deal of *valour* on that occasion.
44. The ascent of Mt. Blanc is attended with no little *peril.*
45. He is a man of very little *discretion.*
46. I am much struck with the *fertility* of the land about here.
47. The story that you heard turned out to be a false *rumour.*
48. He proved to be a very tough *antagonist.*
49. My friend stood by me in all my *troubles.*
50. A prisoner pines in vain for *liberty.*
51. He was kept eight months in *custody.*
52. The *thought* of changing his habits never occurred to him.
53. I have no *objection* to undertake that task.
54. The advice that he gave us deserves careful *thought.*
55. He is subject to *low spirits* at times.
56. What kind of *occupation* does he want?
57. It makes no *matter* what line of life he takes up.
58. The *sweetness* of a rose surpasses that of a tulip.
59. He was made *superintendent* of the works.
60. You have no *business* to come here without leave.
61. There were a great many *buyers* in that bazaar.
62. So far as I know, he has never told an *untruth.*
63. There has been a great *falling off* in the attendance.
64. His spelling was entirely free from *mistakes.*
65. Much *booty* was taken from the captured city.
66. The *gallantry* of the troops astonished every one.
67. You will come to no *harm,* if you stay where you are.
68. I do not want any *apartments* in the top *floor.*

69. He returned to duty on the *expiry* of his leave.
70. The *show* of fancy work was held in that hall.
71. There was an expression of *fear* on every face.
72. The *sum* paid to him came to two pounds ten shillings.
73. A rat is not of the least *service* to man.
74. He shows no *thankfulness* for all that we have done.
75. The sun shone out again in all its *glory*.
76. He found a *pretext* for every wrong thing that he did.
77. After all their talking they came to no *result*.
78. They were soon reduced to a deplorable *state*.
79. There is no *necessity* to say more at present.
80. His *store* of words and phrases is very limited.
81. No progress can be made without *application*.
82. Many bridesmaids were present at the *marriage*.
83. He spoke with a great deal of *assurance*.
84. He raised her with the most tender *solicitude*.
85. The book is not much in *vogue* just now.
86. He had a wonderful *command* of his temper.
87. May I hope for your *forgiveness*?
88. Some of the dumb animals show much *sagacity*.
89. The air is scented with the *perfume* of roses.
90. His *behaviour* this term has been very good.
91. He seems to be an incurable *inebriate*.
92. His vast wealth was an *impediment* to his happiness.
93. Every kind of *obstruction* was put in our way.
94. He spoke very modestly of his own *performances*.
95. At the *close* of his speech he was heartily applauded.
96. One feels a sense of *solitude* in a forest.
97. The *contention* between them was rather acute.
98. Several lives were lost in the *encounter*.
99. The Sultan's army met with a serious *reverse*.
100. There was great *slackness* of discipline.
101. There was much *confusion* in the ranks.
102. He was prompted by *ill-will* to act as he did.
103. He yielded without any sign of *opposition*.
104. I have resigned with very great *unwillingness*.
105. A wise man will avoid *incaution*.
106. This man turned out to be the chief *offender*.

107. An *error* repeated may have serious *consequences*.
108. He had no one to share his *affluence* with him.
109. He always thought of the *welfare* of his country.
110. A great *disaster* had befallen him.
111. Such *pretexts* are despised by every one.
112. His influence is decidedly on the *decline*.
113. His character is not held in much *esteem*.
114. He pays no *heed* to what I tell him.
115. He took up the cause with much *enthusiasm*.
116. My brother is quite an *adept* in rowing.
117. There is a slight *vibration*, when the train passes the house.
118. The rock came down with tremendous *impetus*.
119. There has been rather a marked *depression* in prices.
120. What he said was spoken on the *impulse* of the moment.
121. He is a man of humble *origin*, but of excellent *disposition*.
122. In England the swallow is the *harbinger* of spring.
123. Can you tell me the *source* of all these disputes?
124. He is not acquainted even with the *elements* of the subject.
125. His untimely death was the *destruction* of all my hopes.
126. The enemy carried off a great deal of *plunder*.
127. We have no good road for the *carriage* of goods.
128. Much *alacrity* was shown in removing the luggage.
129. Men will not make good soldiers by *coercion*.
130. It needed very little *exertion* to lift that weight.
131. Cotton *fibre* is warmer than linen.
132. Why should we admit so many *aliens?*
133. I want some kind of *vehicle* to take me home.
134. *Strife* was never known to exist in that house.
135. This rain has done much *harm* to the wheat.
136. There are many *artisans* in this town.
137. Do you understand the *process* of vine-growing?
138. The story is a *fabrication* from beginning to end.
139. *Meddling* generally leads to *muddling*.
140. He lays a great deal of *emphasis* on that word.

141. A. overthrew his *opponent* in wrestling.
142. There was much *destitution* during that long strike.
143. That *malady* is sometimes dangerous.
144. There is no *cure* for the bite of a cobra.
145. He has good reason to be proud of his *forefathers.*
146. I hope to leave a good name to my *posterity.*
147. I have heard that he is of rather low *extraction.*
148. There is no *prospect* of his getting well all at once.
149. One feels a *craving* for fresh fruit in this heat.
150. He fancied he had seen a *spectre.*
151. There was a great *tumult* in the street.
152. Seven men were killed by the *explosion* of a gun.
153. This plant requires some very rich *mould.*
154. The *aspect* of the country is beautiful at this season.
155. There is a *flavour* of something acid in this wine.
156. He applied himself with much *diligence* to his books.
157. I feel no *compassion* for such a man.
158. His manners expose him to much *laughter.*

(*c*) *Substitute another adjective* (*or participle*) *for that italicised in each of the following, taking care that the sense of the sentence remains unaltered* :—

1. The windmill is now entirely *stationary.*
2. The *principal* production of Assam is tea.
3. An honest man is *certain* to be respected.
4. Look at those clouds : a storm appears to *imminent.*
5. He showed *extraordinary* presence of mind that day.
6. He stood alone before the *infuriated* multitude.
7. His demeanour was that of a *calm* and *fearless* man.
8. The explosion was followed by a silence not less *appalling.*
9. To help the poor without hope of a reward is an *unselfish* act.
10. It is not easy to be *cunning* without being *false.*
11. I cannot afford to buy *costly* materials.
12. This news has made me feel very *wretched.*
13. The country looked *desolate* after the famine.
14. A *sly* man does not succeed so well as an *honest* one.

15. We enjoy sailing on *tranquil* waters.
16. Shakspeare is the most *famous* of English poets.
17. Have you brought the *requisite* number of men?
18. It was a *tedious* task, but we accomplished it.
19. We had not money *enough* for our journey.
20. This land is *unproductive;* it yields nothing.
21. An elephant is one of the *shrewdest* of animals.
22. His word is not *trustworthy:* leave him alone.
23. That was an *appropriate* reward for all that he had done.
24. He is rather *timid* and *reserved* in company.
25. It was a *hazardous* thing to do at such a time.
26. You may feel quite *secure;* you have many friends.
27. He was a *fearless* warrior, and fought in many battles.
28. An *immense* wave swept over the ship.
29. The hillside was covered with *profuse* vegetation.
30. He is of rather a *morose* disposition, I fear.
31. It is not *necessary* that the paper should be signed to-day.
32. His gait is ungraceful and his features *unsightly.*
33. Those were not *true* diamonds, but manufactured ones.
34. Pure gold is a very *costly* metal.
35. The *real* facts were very different from the reported ones.
36. A *sincere* friend will help you in time of need.
37. I hope the peace that has been signed will be *permanent.*
38. That will be a *durable* monument to his memory.
39. Practice gives *increased* facility and skill.
40. Have you read the *sad* story contained in that book?
41. He told us the *touching* story of "Paul and Virginia."
42. We all felt *depressed* on hearing it.
43. His manners are anything but *agreeable.*
44. The sweet-*scented* verbena is abundant here.
45. He is a very *painstaking* and *correct* writer.

46. I feel sure that he is a *good-natured* man.
47. Back-biting is a *despicable* vice.
48. The case is *desperate:* we must give it up.
49. We had an *amicable* discussion on that subject.
50. The men who struck work are in a *miserable* plight.
51. Sir Walter Scott was a *famous* poet and novelist.
52. He was *expert* in the use of the bow.
53. A *ready*-witted man is well suited to the bar.
54. This matter was discussed in the *previous* chapter.
55. His style of writing is *deficient* in force.
56. An *easy* command of words is a thing to be *prized.*
57. To know the *exact* force of words is difficult.
58. His command of words is too *scanty* for an orator.
59. He is *painstaking* in everything that he does.
60. The soup to-day is rather *insipid.*
61. *Fresh* air is necessary to health.
62. His speech was not *appropriate* for the audience.
63. The bite of that snake is *innocuous.*
64. He seldom fails to be *humorous* in any company.
65. He had a *robust* faith in the future of South Africa.
66. His *muscular* arms could lift very heavy weights.
67. He had very *onerous* duties to perform.
68. He was a great sufferer, but *uncomplaining* throughout.
69. He was in *abject* bondage to his creditors.
70. He takes a *despondent* view of the situation.
71. A woman of *demure* and retiring manners.
72. Of a *slight* figure and *pensive* expression of face.
73. Of a *frank* disposition and *equable* temper.
74. He is an *ill-mannered* man, and no one likes him.
75. This is a *well-flavoured* dish.
76. She has *winning* manners and a *beautiful* complexion.
77. It was a *clever* device, but it did not *answer.*
78. His conduct has been altogether *irreproachable.*
79. He is a very *competent* teacher, as we all know.
80. A *sallow* complexion is not one to be admired.
81. His face looked *thin* and *careworn.*

82. He returned from the tropics with a *tanned* complexion.

83. He was *slovenly* in his dress on most occasions.

84. It was a *lucky* thing for him that he was not caught.

85. Even in a *drooping* rose there is some beauty.

86. His voice is *husky*, not so clear as usual.

87. Horse-chestnuts are not at all *rare* in England.

88. *Standing* water soon becomes *impure.*

89. He stood as *still* as a statue.

90. Let us have the rooms well *ventilated.*

91. His step was so *stealthy* that no one heard him coming.

92. He is very *stubborn:* you will not convince him.

93. He is too *impetuous* to be relied on for prudence.

94. *Total* abstinence from wine is necessary to some.

95. His daily habits were *detrimental* to his health.

96. His activity is *amazing:* he never seems *tired.*

97. He carried on a very *thriving* trade.

98. His mind was *undisturbed* through all his difficulties.

99. Her mind, however, was much *agitated.*

100. He was *provident* in all his habits.

101. He is a *vigorous* worker, and is *sure* to prosper.

102. Such a thing as failure is very *improbable.*

103. A squirrel is an *agile* little animal.

104. He is a man of *inflexible* will.

105. Ants and bees are both *diligent* workers.

106. A wolf has a *voracious* appetite.

107. I am quite *prepared* for any emergency.

108. I am not *unmindful* of all that I owe to you.

109. He was rather *down-hearted* at the state of affairs.

110. Any *well-known* object will do for an object-lesson.

111. That was a *forcible* argument; it convinced me.

112. We felt a slight *vibratory* motion in the ground.

113. The horse was galloping at a *furious* pace.

114. No *sound* reason could be given for his conduct.

115. The river fell upon the fields with *overwhelming* force.

116. The *diurnal* motion of the earth takes up twenty-four hours.

117. Make the best you can of the *fleeting* moment.

118. The illness has become *chronic*, I am afraid.

119. His health is always *precarious.*

120. I have a *fervid* dislike to *disingenuous* professions.

121. A stag is one of the *fleetest* of animals.

122. He was a man of *unvarying* honesty.

123. I fear he is rather *indolent* by nature.

124. I am *inquisitive* to hear the last news.

125. Avoid the use of *redundant* words.

126. The part that he played was very *ludicrous.*

127. A *concise* narrative is all that is needed.

128. He is a very *fluent* speaker.

129. The prisoner escaped by a *subterranean* passage.

130. Astronomy is the study of the *celestial* bodies.

131. He told us a *laughable* story about himself.

132. He drives with rather too *loose* a rein.

133. He is a very *droll* man, and makes every one laugh.

134. It was a *dismal* day for going on a journey.

135. The colour of your dress has become very *dingy.*

136. His origin, I hear, was rather *plebeian.*

137. He is a *zealous* supporter of the cause of temperance.

138. A *sprightly* manner helps to make others gay.

139. That was a *foul* stroke, as the umpire declared.

140. There is no *hidden* meaning behind the words he used.

141. The air of this place is very *health-giving.*

142. I am not *disposed* to make any more changes.

143. His meaning is quite *obvious.*

144. His healthy appearance is *illusory.*

145. There is a smell of something *rancid* in this room.

146. He liked to be surrounded by *fawning* courtiers.

147. Johnson was a man of *serious* disposition.

148. He was *humane* in his treatment of the prisoners.

149. His conduct is not more *harsh* than it ought to be.

150. He is rather too *frivolous* to make a good officer.

(*d*) *Substitute another adverb for that italicised in each of the following sentences, taking care that the sense of the sentence remains unaltered*:—

1. The law *recently* passed will place some check on drunkenness.
2. The explanation given is *quite* satisfactory.
3. Except for his help, we should *undoubtedly* have perished.
4. They all felt that they had been *fairly* and even *handsomely* treated.
5. He acted very *indiscreetly* in that matter.
6. He spoke very *discourteously* to his betters.
7. The name of that student was *purposely* omitted.
8. Those children were *meagrely* fed and *scantily* clad.
9. He is *seldom* absent from his proper place.
10. The thief was *rigorously* punished.
11. He was *gravely* cautioned against such imprudence.
12. He turned up *unexpectedly* at 6 o'clock.
13. The boat sailed *merrily* along on the placid lake.
14. The town consists *principally* of mechanics.
15. He *generally* comes home by 5 P.M.
16. He is *manifestly* hiding the truth from us.
17. You must start *immediately*; the time is up.
18. His essay, though short, is *correctly* worded and *well* arranged.
19. He spoke out *bravely*, and was attentively listened to.
20. He was very *severely* handled by the enemy.
21. He is *unusually* attentive to his work.
22. The man was *fiercely* attacked by a bull.
23. He is very *busily* engaged in digging his garden.
24. The bear walks along very *awkwardly*.
25. He *angrily* told the vagrant to leave the house.
26. He has *repeatedly* been cautioned before.
27. He was *mortally* wounded in that encounter
28. I spent an hour very *agreeably* in his garden.

29. I thank you most *heartily* for what you have done.
30. He seized the oar and pulled it *lustily*.
31. My luck that day was *particularly* bad.
32. It was *solely* with this object that I came here.
33. The river winds *sluggishly* through the fields.
34. The waters flow *noiselessly* along.
35. He *indignantly* refused to accept the excuse.
36. He has worked most *assiduously* all day.
37. He told me my faults very *candidly*.
38. He behaved *perfidiously* to his oldest friend.
39. *Doubtlessly* the sinner will have his reward.
40. He *basely* deserted the cause entrusted to him.
41. He *warmly* supported the cause of temperance.
42. He spoke very *humbly* of his own abilities.
43. The debt was *grudgingly* paid up at last.
44. They were all *gaily* dressed for the ceremony.
45. We cannot be *legitimately* excluded.
46. He writes *indifferently* and spells worse.
47. I am not *thoroughly* acquainted with the rules.
48. He went about the business very *charily*.

SECTION 2.—TO DISCRIMINATE WORDS NEARLY ALLIED IN MEANING.

80. Discrimination of Words.—Though it is possible in certain contexts, as we have shown in the previous section, to use one word for another without discriminating the different shades of meaning that may exist between them, yet in other contexts such discrimination is necessary, and when properly carried out, adds much to the merit of composition. We now give a few examples.

Exercise on § 80. (To be done orally and at sight.)

Fill up the gaps, taking care to use the right word in the right place:—

aware / conscious — He was well —— of the difficulties to be overcome, and yet —— of his own inability to overcome them.

needs / desires — A miser can easily satisfy his ——, but can never satisfy his ——.

booty / prey — The farms became the —— of the invaders, who carried off much ——.

cure / remedy — The doctor tried one —— after another, but failed to discover a real ——.

5. custom / habit — A —— of industry leads to the —— of keeping punctual hours.

famous / notorious — The hermit was as —— for his good deeds, as the robber was —— for his evil ones.

meaning / import — The —— which the writer intends us to see in his words does not tally with their real ——.

observe / remark — I have had many opportunities of —— his character, but I never —— that particular trait.

invent / discover — Vaccination was —— in England; printing was —— in China.

10. large / great — India is a —— country, containing many —— cities.

stop / stay — Let us —— on the way at this hotel, and —— here for the night.

unlikely / improbable — It is —— that this will happen. The story we have heard seems very ——.

faults / defects — The —— that he has committed are owing to certain serious —— in his character.

strict / severe — He was as —— in observing the rules as he was —— in punishing a breach of them.

15. disorder, confusion — There is as much —— in his ideas as there is —— in the arrangement of his books.

divide, separate — Society is —— into several different classes. The lowest is —— from the highest by a wide interval.

divulge, reveal — That secret must not be —— at present, and even when it has been, it must not be —— and made public property.

duty, obligation — It is the —— of A. to support his own parent; but he has not entered into any —— to support his neighbour's parent.

ease, facility — By dint of practice he has now acquired —— in the use of tools, and he can make almost anything with ——.

20. empty, vacant — As soon as a seat in Parliament becomes ——, he hopes to get in and assume the —— title of M.P.

example, instance — I know an —— of a step-mother, who is an —— of kindness to her step-children.

fruitful, fertile — The soil of this orchard is so ——, that the apple-trees are —— without any cultivation.

fluctuate, waver — The reason why he —— so much in action is that his mind —— between one motive and another.

frail, brittle — A reed is so —— that it can be easily broken in two; glass is so —— that, when it is broken, it separates into several pieces.

25. give, grant — We —— his request and —— him something more besides.

gratitude, thankfulness — He felt much —— for the kindness he had received, and showed it by the —— that he expressed.

guiltless / innocent
He is a man of —— life, and I feel sure he is —— of the offence imputed him.

gather / conjecture
I can —— your age from your appearance, but without seeing you I could not —— what your age is.

impossible / impracticable
The plan that you propose is so expensive as to be ——, though, if we had the means, there is nothing —— about it.

30. enlarge / increase
By —— a student's mind, you —— his stock of knowlege, and stimulate his powers of observation.

intention / purpose
It is not my —— to abandon the —— that I have formed.

old / aged
He is an —— friend of mine, about forty-five years of age; and his —— father is still living.

vain / proud
My son is not —— of his recent success, although I am a little —— of it myself.

part / portion
The estate was divided into four ——, and each of the heirs received his ——.

35. eldest / oldest
My —— son is sixteen years of age; he is the —— boy in the school.

fade / wither
In autumn the flowers begin to ——, and the leaves to ——.

liberty / freedom
The prisoners were set at ——; they have now perfect —— to go where they like.

new / fresh
The —— turn that affairs have taken gives us —— courage.

bad / wicked
A man who leads a —— life has a —— prospect before him.

40. strong / powerful
A —— constitution is a —— incentive to work.

	Words	Sentence
	healthy wholesome	A —— diet helps to make a man ——.
	further farther	I cannot go any ——. My house is —— from London than yours is.
	enormous immense	The elephant is an —— beast, and in Central Africa has an —— tract of country to graze in.
	timid cowardly	Though he was by nature a —— man, he repelled that —— assault with courage.
45.	amusement recreation	Football is a very good kind of —— for boys in the winter, and it is some —— to spectators to watch a good match.
	approval approbation	The —— of a man's own conscience is more satisfactory than the —— of the public.
	glad gratified	I am —— to hear that your son has arrived safely from New Zealand, and am —— to know that he inquired so kindly after me.
	desert abandon	All hope of rescue was ——, when the life-boat —— us.
	forgive pardon	A person may —— a fault; but a court of justice cannot —— a criminal.
50.	faith confidence	I have —— in the ultimate triumph of good over evil, but no —— in the usefulness of this particular law.
	compunction remorse	He felt no —— at the time of doing the deed, but felt the keenest —— afterwards.
	force authority	By sheer —— of character he has acquired more —— than he possesses by right.

anger resentment	Though he showed a great deal of —— at the time, he has no feeling of —— now.
build erect	He has —— a cycle-shed at the back of the house which he —— last year.
55. attribute impute	It is more charitable to —— proper motives, when this is possible, than to —— bad ones.
avenge revenge	He —— the wrongs done to his parents, but he did not —— himself upon his enemies.
amicable friendly	He was always —— in his intercourse with me; but when I needed his help, he was not ——.
answer reply	He sent a —— to my letter; but this contained no —— to my question.
affliction grief	We have suffered a great deal of —— in our recent ——.
60. advance proceed	He —— on his journey, but he had not —— far, before he was again stopped.
alter change	To —— a dress is to put on another: to —— one is to make it different in some respects from what it was.
ancient antique	A temple built a great many centuries ago is said to be ——; a modern temple built in the style of an ancient one is said to be ——.
applaud praise	He was —— for rescuing the drowning child, and every one —— his bravery.
arms weapons	As he had no ——, he seized the poker and tongs, which he used as ——.
65. attempt try	If you fail when you make your first ——, do not despair, but —— again.

	Words	Sentence
	bashful modest	A. is so —— that he avoids society: B. does not avoid society, but he is very —— about his own merits.
	trifling trivial	The sum of money at stake was ——, but the principle involved was anything but ——.
	transitory fleeting	Life is but ——: let us therefore make the best use of the —— hour.
	generous liberal	He was —— with his purse, and had —— feelings towards all men.
70.	serious solemn	He made a —— promise that he would give his most —— attention to the matter.
	sympathy compassion	From feelings of —— with human suffering he showed a great deal of —— towards the needy.
	idle lazy	Though we had no desire to be ——, we have had rather an —— time of late owing to scarcity of orders.
	character reputation	One, whose —— is bad at heart, may yet manage to make for himself a good ——.
	effective effectual	The medicine that he prescribed is said to be ——, but it did not in my case work an —— remedy.
75.	confess admit	The prisoner, before his execution, —— that he had committed the crime, and —— the justice of the sentence.
	crime sin	The —— was against the laws of the country; the same act regarded as a breach of God's laws may be called a ——.
	fit suitable	He was a very —— man for the post, but he accepted it on terms that were not —— for a man of his rank.

religious righteous	He is —— in his conduct towards God, and —— in his dealings with men.
deference respect	I cannot show much —— to any one for whom I feel no ——.
80. learning wisdom	So far as —— is concerned, he is well versed in books; but he shows little —— in the practical affairs of life.
understand apprehend	I —— the general drift of his letter, but could not —— that particular point.
return replace	You must —— the book that you borrowed, and —— the one that you have lost.
event occurrence	The —— is very much what we expected, though its —— has been rather late.
below beneath	He is a little —— me in social rank, but not by any means —— me in character.
85. bestow confer	The king —— the rank of knighthood upon A., and —— several favours on B.
brave courageous	A. is so —— that he thinks nothing of the danger; B. is aware of the danger, but —— enough to face it.
bring fetch	Be so good as to —— the book lying on the table beside you. I will —— the footstool from the next room.
burden load	The camel received the —— on its back, and was well able to bear the ——.
inclination disposition	A. is of a worse —— than B., for the latter has no —— to circulate the slander which A. has both invented and circulated.

90. cause / reason — A fair wind is the —— of the vessel's sailing: the order of the captain is the —— of its sailing to-day.

clothe / dress — Savages —— themselves in skins; moderns —— according to the prevailing fashion.

complete / entire — He travelled over the —— continent; but his book of travels is not ——, because it has no maps.

conciliate / reconcile — He —— both of them to himself; but he was not able to —— one disputant to the other.

conflict / contest — There was a severe —— at the election; but there was no —— or disturbance between the rival factions.

95. conquer / overcome — In his march over the Alps Hannibal —— every difficulty, but he did not succeed in —— the Italians.

contented / satisfied — The poor are often ——, but a miser is never ——. He never thinks that he has enough.

convince / persuade — He is very clever in —— people to act in a certain way, but does not succeed equally well in —— their reason.

contiguous / adjacent — A.'s house is —— to mine; B.'s stands in an —— field, about ten yards off.

copy / imitate — He —— the words of that letter correctly; but whenever he attempts to —— the style of the writer in composing a letter of his own, he fails.

100. credit / trust — I —— him with the best intentions, and —— that he will not disappoint me.

ridicule / derision — I do not mind a little —— if I make a mistake; but I dislike —— whether I have made a mistake or not.

invalid / patient — For some time past my son has been one of Dr. C.'s —— : I hope he will not become a confirmed ——.

irksome / tedious — A task is —— when you have no taste for it, and —— when it is long and monotonous.

lament / deplore — His death was —— with many expressions of sorrow, and —— in silence by all who knew him.

105. leave / quit — He —— the house at 4 A.M., and I believe he has —— it for ever.

liable / subject — He is so —— to sickness, that he is —— to the loss of his appointment.

likely / probable — What you have told us does not seem at all —— ; but if any one is —— to know, you are.

little / small — A —— pony has —— chance of keeping pace with a big horse.

method / style — The —— in which the book has been written is excellent, and the —— in which the subject has been worked out does credit to the author.

110. modern / recent — —— studies have been much recommended in —— years.

need / necessity — There is no —— to refer to the subject again, until the —— of action arises.

news / tidings — We have received no —— of his safe arrival. There is no —— of importance in to-day's paper.

new / novel — We commenced the —— year with a —— kind of experience.

obstinate / stubborn — The one is too —— to act against his own judgment; the other is as —— as a horse that will not move on.

115. peaceable / peaceful { Being of a —— disposition he lives a —— life.

place / put { Let this plant be —— in a flower-pot and —— in the drawing-room.

protect / defend { Kimberley was —— by its guns, and —— by its garrison and by the inhabitants.

raise / lift { He —— the child that had fallen, and —— it up in his arms.

rational / reasonable { A —— course of action is what we expect from a —— being.

120. rebuke / reproof { He listened patiently to the —— administered to him; for he was conscious of having deserved ——.

receive / accept { This box is scarcely large enough to —— all the presents that you have —— from your friends.

repeal / revoke { A judge may —— a sentence, but he cannot —— a law; only parliament can do the last.

satiate / satisfy { They had had enough and were ——; others had had a little too much and were ——.

slake / quench { With this bottle of water we three can —— our thirst, but not —— it.

125. uncertain / doubtful { Men are —— how to act when they are —— what is going to happen.

union / unity { Though there is outward —— in that sect, there is not much —— of feeling amongst the members.

unsettled / distracted { His mind has been so much —— by constant worries, that it has become too —— to attend to anything.

untruth lie	We give the name of —— to what is said falsely in jest; and the name of —— to what is said falsely with an evil purpose.
worthless unworthy	His statement is —— of consideration, in fact utterly ——.
130. employ use	He —— his opportunities to great advantage, and —— a large number of hands to get the work done.
utility usefulness	The —— of the discovery of the power of steam has been proved by the —— of the numberless machines that are worked by steam.
worth value	The —— of this horse is what it will sell for; its ——, while it remains in your possession, depends upon the amount and kind of work it does for you.
warn caution	He was —— of the approach of the express train, and —— against standing too near the edge of the platform.
whole entire	I wished to read the —— book; but the volume was not ——, as some pages had been lost.

SECTION 3.—TO SUPPLY THE OPPOSITES TO GIVEN WORDS.

81. Words and their Opposites.—Almost every word in common use has an opposite. In fact we cannot well understand what a word means unless we can name some other word that gives an opposite or at least a very different meaning. Thus, if we say that we are ashamed of a thing, this is another way of saying that we are in a mood the opposite to that of being proud of it.

Exercise on § 81. (To be done orally and at sight.)

Fill up the gap with a word expressing the opposite to the word italicised[1] :—

1. An *open* enemy is better than a —— one who pretends to be a friend.
2. Instead of helping me *forward* he dragged me ——.
3. A *friend* in *name*, but an —— in ——.
4. A *dull* morning sometimes ends in a —— day.
5. A *radiant* sunshine was followed by a —— sunset.
6. *More* haste may end in —— speed.
7. He remained in *bondage*, till —— was granted him.
8. *Civility* makes no enemies, as —— does.
9. Honest *poverty* is better than dishonest ——.
10. His manners are *rough*, not at all ——.
11. A *well-bred* man cannot be wholly ——.
12. He is a *superficial*, not a —— thinker.
13. This house has been *substantially*, not —— built.
14. *Adversity* tries a man's character as much as ——.
15. The one lives in *hope*, the other sinks into ——.
16. There is an *abundance* of fruit-trees, but a —— of fruit.
17. Avoid a man who is brave in *words*, but not in ——.
18. *Long* were their speeches, —— were their subscriptions.
19. His face is more *repulsive* than ——.
20. An *idle* student does not progress so well as an —— one.
21. The *innocent* often suffer for the ——.
22. He was *slow* in debate, but —— in action.
23. A man of smooth temper, but —— manners.
24. He was always *hard-working*, never —— in anything.
25. That day of *gloom* was succeeded by one of ——.

---

[1] In doing this exercise it is not enough to set the negative form of a word against the positive. Thus for the opposite to *careful* a student should be expected to give such a word as *negligent*, and not the merely negative form *careless*.

26. It is better to *laugh* than to —— in time of trouble.
27. There were more *sellers* than —— in that bazaar.
28. In a railway accident *absence* of *body* is better than —— of ——.
29. The *winner* gained less than the —— lost.
30. *Cruelty* and —— cannot exist together.
31. A dead *silence* is even more oppressive than ——.
32. The *ebb* and —— of the sea tide are unceasing.
33. *Ancient* history pleases me more than ——.
34. Some *hurried*, others —— on the road.
35. The one *receded* as fast as the other ——.
36. Is it *thawing* to-day, or is it —— ?
37. The *victories* of Pyrrhus were more like ——.
38. His *departure* took place an hour after his ——.
39. *Pleasure* is generally mixed with some degree of ——.
40. His *guilt* was more easy of proof than his ——.
41. To err is *human*; to forgive ——.
42. It is easier to *descend* than to —— a steep bank.
43. In *sickness* no less than in —— he was fond of reading.
44. His energies were aroused more by *failure* than by ——.
45. *Truth* is stranger than ——.
46. I cannot *remember* anything that you ——.
47. On *ignorance*, not on ——, his hopes are based.
48. The *love* of *right* is equivalent to the —— of ——.
49. *Economy* must recover what —— has lost.
50. Cork *floats*, while iron —— in water.
51. I prefer a *thin* soup to a —— one.
52. It is better to be *demure* than —— in manner.
53. His dress was always *neat*, never ——.
54. This orange is *juicy*, that was a —— one.
55. A *sweet* apple agrees with me, a —— one does not.
56. *Modesty* is more attractive than ——.
57. The *increase* of goods was followed by a —— of prices.
58. The towns *prospered*, while agriculture ——.

59. Some flowers *bloomed*, while others ——.
60. The *supply* increased, but the —— fell.
61. Even towards the *miserly* he was ——.
62. *Passive*, not ——, resistance is what he decided on.
63. It is better to be *provident* than ——.
64. A *genial* manner makes more friends than a—— one.
65. This soil is *barren* rather than ——.
66. What I said was said *in jest*, not ——.
67. A less *rigid* and more —— rule is needed.
68. His manners are as *repulsive* as her's are ——.
69. *Permanent*, not ——, help is necessary.
70. An *artificial* diamond is worth less than a —— one.
71. The voyage out was *smooth*, the return passage was ——.
72. *Reluctantly*, not at all ——, he gave his consent.
73. We want *systematic*, not ——, work.
74. He prefers *concealing* to —— his thoughts.
75. He spoke *positively*, not ——, on that matter.
76. I am more *averse* to that plan than —— to it.
77. He is too *hasty*, not —— enough, in his purchases.
78. He expressed himself *distinctly*, by no means ——.
79. The message was *written*, not ——.
80. The tide *recedes* more than it ——.
81. He has *retrograded*, not ——, in his studies.
82. Music does not *lower*, but ——, the feelings.
83. *Voluntary* service is more effective than ——.
84. He is too *meek* to cope with such a —— man.
85. A *far-seeing* man succeeds, a —— one fails.
86. *Seize* an opportunity, or it will be ——.
87. All music, both *sacred* and ——, delights me.
88. A writer who is *clear*, not ——, gives most pleasure.
89. His figure, far from being *bent*, is very ——.
90. *Generous* in his professions, —— in his actions.
91. The *crafty* man deceived his —— customer.
92. He gave a *straightforward*, not a ——, answer.
93. He is *reckless*, not at all ——, in his expenditure.
94. This work *deadens* his wits: we must try to —— them.

95. A man should be *ashamed* of his *ignorance* rather than —— of his ——.

96. There is an *abundance* of work, but a —— of workmen.

97. *Abhorrence* of *falsehood* implies a —— of ——.

98. Was your friend *acquitted* or was he —— of that charge?

99. *Avoid* that which is *evil*; —— that which is ——.

100. One man expressed his *assent*; another his ——.

101. Such a proceeding is more *adverse* than —— to progress.

102. Cowardice is an *incentive*, not a ——, to falsehood.

103. I am more *angry* with him than ——.

104. *Send away* this workman, and —— the other.

105. Some patients change for the *better*, others for the ——.

106. He was *careful* of his money, but —— of his time.

107. I did this not by *accident*, but by ——.

108. A. *complied with* my instructions; B. —— them.

109. One man *concurred*, the other ——, with me.

110. He came back *within* the time, you —— it.

111. The king *confided in* his ministers; but they —— the king.

112. His opinion does not *coincide*, but ——, with mine.

113. What is one man's *meat* is another's ——.

114. He was *deaf* to my entreaties, but —— to yours.

115. His style was *abundant* in words, but —— in ideas.

116. A *deficiency* of moisture is more to be feared than an ——.

117. What *augments* your profits —— mine.

118. Better to *die* by the sword than —— by treachery.

119. He *differs* with me, but —— with you.

120. I was *disappointed* rather than —— with him.

121. The meanings of these words have been *confused* rather than ——.

122. The one filled me with *disgust*, the other with ——.

123. The king did not *conciliate*, but ——, his people.

124. I shall *take up* the project that you have ——.

125. He is an *unskilful* cricketer, while you are very ——.

126. A *graceful* player is more admired than a —— one.

127. His thoughts are never *concentrated*, always ——.

128. *Home* industries should be encouraged more than —— ones.

129. *Wild* flowers are sometimes as pretty as —— ones.

130. I trust his *frowns* sooner than his ——.

131. You are *forced* to *stay*, I am —— to ——.

132. Are you *glad* or —— for what you have done?

133. They *rejoiced* more than they —— at his misfortunes.

134. He *opposed* more frequently than he —— me.

135. A *harsh* temper may co-exist with a —— voice.

136. Their *hostility* is less to be feared than their ——.

137. He was less *comforted* than —— on hearing the news.

138. He did what was *obstructive* rather than —— to peace.

139. I have *suffered* from that by which you have ——.

140. It is more blessed to *give* than to —— (*New Test.*).

141. In all labour there is *profit*; but the talk of the lips tendeth only to —— (*Old Test.*).

142. One *rises*, another ——: one *succeeds*, another ——.

143. The *proud* man was at last subdued by the ——.

144. He *exasperated* me instead of —— me.

145. There is no music in *discord*, only in ——.

146. His debts were *reduced*, and his income ——, by one quarter.

147. I have more *contempt* than —— for his character.

148. *Resemblances* strike me more readily than ——.

149. One *instigates* him to do it; the other —— him.

150. He is versed in the *principles*, not the ——, of trade.

151. *Fools* build houses for —— to live in.

152. I wish to *retain* the power which you are ready to ——.

Section 4.—To supply Words formed with Affixes.

82. Use of Affixes in Composition.—An affix is a letter, syllable, or word that is placed either before or after some radical word in order to modify its meaning. One placed before is called a prefix, as "*sub*-judge"; one placed after is called a suffix, as "fathom-*less*." In the practice of composition a knowledge of prefixes and suffixes enables us to express by a single word what would otherwise have to be expressed by several words. Thus by the help of the prefix *sub*- we can form the word "subjudge," for which we should otherwise be forced to use the roundabout phrase "a judge holding a rank lower than that of some other judge." Similarly, by the help of the suffix *-less* we can form the word "fathomless," which saves us from using the lengthy and less convenient phrase "that cannot be fathomed." We will now give a few examples of those affixes that are more especially useful in this respect.[1]

Excess.—**Over-.** The meat has been *over*-cooked (cooked more than it should have been).

Defect.—**Under-.** The meat is *under*-done (cooked less than it should have been).

[1] For a more complete account of suffixes and prefixes the student must go to any of the standard grammars. In this place we have mentioned only those that are especially useful in enabling us to express by a *single* word what would otherwise have to be expressed by several.

Reversal.—**Dis-, de-, un-.** He *dis*-mounted (came down from the horse which he had previously mounted). The king was *de*-throned (removed from the throne which he had formerly occupied). He was *un*-seated (he lost the seat on which he had formerly sat).

Slightly.— **-ish, sub-.** His complexion is pal-*ish* (rather pale). The fruit is *sub*-acid (slightly acid).

Of lower rank.—**Under-, sub-.** He is the *under*-secretary (the assistant secretary, of lower rank than the chief secretary). A *sub*-judge (a judge below some other judge).

Loss of Office.—**Ex-.** The *ex*-emperor of the French (one who was once emperor, but has ceased to be so).

In the place of.—**Vice-.** The *vice*-roy of India (one who rules India in place of, or as representative of, the king).

To an extreme degree.—**Ultra-.** He is an *ultra*-Liberal (one who holds extreme views as a Liberal politician).

Self.—**Auto-.** An *auto*-car (a self-moved car, not drawn by a horse). *Auto*-biography (life self-written).

Surpassing.—**Out-.** The sun *out*-shines the stars (shines more brightly than the stars so as to render them invisible).

Before.—**Pre-, ante-.** He *pre*-occupied the seat (occupied the seat before any one else did). This is only an *ante*-room (a room before or leading to another room).

After.—**Post-, after-.** I must add a *post*-script (something written after the letter has been finished). This was an *after*-thought (a thought which came into the mind after something had been said or done).

Up.—**Ad-.** Let us *a*(*d*)-scend this hill (climb up this hill). *Ac*(*d*)-clivity, the upward slope.

Down.—**De-.** Let us now *de*-scend the hill (come down the hill). *De*-clivity, the downward slope.

The price paid.— **-age.** What is the post-*age* (the price of the stamp to be used for posting the letter)?

Causing a thing.—**Be-, -en, en-, -fy, -ise.** The sea is now *be*-calmed (made calm or caused to be calm). Let us dark-*en* the room (make the room dark). He was *en*-deared to me (made dear to me). The colour was intensi-*fied* (made more intense). This will fertil-*ise* the soil (make the soil more fertile).

Afresh.—**Re-.** The classes must be *re*-formed (formed afresh, formed over again. When *re* is used for this purpose, it must be followed by a hyphen. There is a great difference in meaning between *re-form* and *reform*).

Exercise on § 82. (To be done orally and at sight.)

Express by single words the phrases italicised in the following sentences:—

1. Your painting seems to have been *insufficiently coloured.*
2. The soul is *separated from the body* by death.
3. Your box *weighs more than* mine.
4. He *made a lower bid than I did* in that auction.
5. The meeting must appoint a *man who will act as chairman when the regular chairman is absent.*
6. He is a *man of extreme Protestant views.*
7. They climbed the *upward slope* with much labour.
8. He *judged* the case *before hearing the evidence.*
9. The sheep must be *counted all over again.*
10. These heavy clouds *make* the atmosphere *dark.*
11. There was a splendid *glow after the sun had gone down.*
12. This clay ought to *make* the bank *solid.*
13. He must be *granted an indemnity* for his losses.
14. *Give* the letter *a date subsequent to that on which the letter is written.*
15. I prefer a *biography written by the man himself.*

16. What ought we to pay as *fee to the broker?*

17. He was appointed *to act for the chancellor in his absence.*

18. The fruit has become more *ripe than it should be.*

19. The *second mowing of the grass* was a fine crop this season.

20. Her eyes were *made dim* with tears.

21. We *defeated* him *by a majority of votes.*

22. Napoleon III., *after he had ceased to be emperor* of France, spent the rest of his days in England.

23. They *had formed an unfavourable judgment beforehand* against the plan.

24. The doll must now be *dressed over again.*

25. The witness was *reduced to a state of terror.*

26. This article is *offered for sale at less than its proper price.*

27. The facts have been *stated in terms exceeding the truth.*

28. The *downward slope* of the hill will give us no trouble.

29. The *cost of posting* this letter was rather high.

30. Nothing will *make* taxation *popular.*

31. These legends must be *put on a rational basis.*

32. A. *grew taller than* his elder brother.

33. He will *bid more than* you for that article.

34. This *contract* is *subordinate to another contract.*

35. You must *remove the bolt of* that door.

36. He was *thrown off his horse* and had a bad fall.

37. He is entitled to *be paid something while he halts.*

38. I want to see his *own handwriting.*

39. He is an *extreme Conservative* in politics.

40. Silver has been *brought down to a lower price* by a rise in the value of gold.

41. The rule, though now obsolete, must be *introduced afresh.*

42. The *hours following noon* will be spent at home.

43. His hands were *reduced to a state of numbness.*

44. Let the letter be *dated before the actual date of writing.*

45. He is the *assistant to the principal editor* of the journal.

46. We must *remove the deception under which he labours.*

47. He has been *relieved of the illusion which had taken hold of his mind.*

48. I have *let* the house *to a man who will pay me the rent that I shall pay to the landlord.*

49. The poor boy has *not had enough food to eat.*

50. He has been *more anxious than he need have been* about that matter.

51. This is one of the *smaller divisions* of the book.

52. His rank is that of *one next below the prefect.*

53. He is of a *rather red* complexion.

54. We must *get rid of the odour in* this room.

55. Dr. J., *formerly bishop* of Calcutta, has returned to England on account of age.

56. He was appointed *to act in the place of admiral.*

57. He *received the power* to act as he did.

58. What shall we have to pay *for using the wharf?*

59. He will be *deprived of the weapons with which he armed himself.*

60. This is the *secondary title* of the book.

61. There were several huge animals *before the deluge.*

62. He *made slaves of* the unfortunate negroes.

63. Such injustice *fills* one's mind *with bitterness.*

64. This *gives him a title* to better treatment.

65. They have *left the ship on which they had embarked.*

66. This event *makes* our position *dangerous.*

67. *A man of extreme Radical views* has been elected.

68. His hands are so *engrained with grime* that they need hot water and soap.

69. The fox has *gone out of sight* all of a sudden.

70. The table must *have a fresh covering put on it.*

71. His language should be *recast in modern form.*

72. I *supposed* that he was wrong *before I was told.*

73. The son *is heavier than* his father.

74. The subject *has been entangled and must be cleared up.*

75. The water at present is *too hot for the purpose.*

76 The men are *paid less than they ought to be.*

77. The cost was *estimated above what was reasonable.*

78. No one sees *a garment that is worn under other garments.*

79. The wall looks *rather grey* with age.

80. The *lady who was once Empress of the French* survived her husband by many years.

81. The room must be *cleared of the infection.*

82. The tone of the book is *more than usually sentimental.*

83. The vagrant must be *removed from the place where he has lodged.*

SECTION 5.—TO SUPPLY PREPOSITIONS AFTER CERTAIN WORDS.

83. How Prepositions are used.—A preposition expresses some kind of relation between two different things. The word denoting one of the things is called the Object. The word denoting the other thing may be a noun, or a verb, or an adjective, or an adverb. The selection of the preposition to be used in any given example depends partly on the character of the relation which the writer and speaker desires to express, and partly on idiom or custom.

Exercises on § 83. (To be done orally and at sight.)

(*a*) *Fill up the gap in each sentence with the appropriate preposition:*—

Accompanied *with, by.* His speech was accompanied —— a bow. He was accompanied —— his dog.

Accord *with, to.* He acted in accordance —— instructions. According —— what you tell me he must be very clever.

Accountable *to, for.* He is accountable —— the government —— his actions.

Adapted *to, for.* The plan that you propose is well adapted —— my abilities, but not —— the purpose that I have in hand.

Advantage *of*, *over*. He has the advantage —— me (*Definite article*). He has an advantage —— me (*Indef. art.*).

Agree *to*, *with*. I cannot agree —— you (person) on that subject, nor do I agree —— your proposals (thing).

Angry *at*, *with*, *for*. He is angry —— me (person) —— having made that remark; and I am angry —— his rudeness (thing).

Annoyed *with*, *at*. He was much annoyed —— his accusers (person); and still more annoyed —— their dishonesty (thing).

Answer *to*, *for*. You will have to answer —— your employer —— such neglect of duty.

Appeal *to*, *for*, *against*. I appeal —— you —— redress —— such injustice.

Arrive *at*, *in*. He has arrived —— Dover (smaller space). He has arrived —— Italy (larger space).

Attend *to*, *on*, *at*. Your attendance —— the committee is necessary. Your attendance —— the committee-room is necessary. You must attend —— the book.

Attended *with*, *by*. The proceedings were attended —— more noise than there should have been. He was attended —— two friends (agent).

Authority *over*, *on*, *for*. He is my authority —— saying so. He is a good authority —— that subject. He has no authority —— the committee.

Beg *of*, *for*, *from*. Let me beg pardon —— you. I beg —— a little encouragement —— you.

Betrayed *to*, *into*. The city was betrayed —— the enemy. It was betrayed —— the hands of the enemy.

Blessed *in*, *with*. He is blessed —— good health, and blessed —— his children.

Blind *of*, *to*. He was blind —— one eye. He was blind —— the consequences of his own folly.

Blush *at*, *for*. I blush —— the good name that you have lost. I blush —— your folly.

Break *into, through, of, to, with.* I have broken —— him once for all. Who will break the news —— her? Try to break yourself —— that habit. He broke —— all restraint. A thief broke —— the house.

Bring *to, under.* We must bring this matter —— light. It must be brought —— discussion.

Burst *into, upon.* He burst —— the country with an overwhelming force. He burst —— a rage.

Call *on, to, for.* I called —— him to come. We must call —— our new neighbour. This matter calls —— prompt action.

Care *of, for.* I do not care —— him at all. The care —— the house does not rest with me.

Careful *of, about.* He is very careful —— what he eats. He was careful —— his money.

Cause *of, for.* There is no cause —— anxiety. What was the cause —— his anxiety?

Change *to, for.* He has changed a good deal —— the worse. Give me change —— sixpence. Change this sixpenny piece —— coppers.

Charge *to, with.* The gun is charged (loaded) —— a bullet. You are charged (entrusted) —— this business. You are charged (accused) —— a crime. This must be charged —— your account.

Claim *to, on* or *against.* I have a claim —— you. I have a claim —— better treatment.

Clamorous *for, against.* They are clamorous —— better pay. They are clamorous —— his exactions.

Clothed *in, with.* The rich man, though clothed —— fine linen, was clothed —— shame.

Come *across, into, by, of, to.* This has come —— fashion. How did he come —— (acquire) all this money? This comes —— being lazy. The total comes —— four pounds. I came —— him (accidentally met him) yesterday.

Communicate *with, on, to.* I will communicate —— him —— the subject (*Intrans.*). I will communicate my views —— him (*Trans.*).

Compare *with*, *to*. We may compare apples —— pears (similars compared). Genius may be compared —— a lightning-flash (dissimilars compared).

Compete *with* or *against*, *for*. He competed —— me —— a scholarship.

Complain *of*, *to*, *against*, *about*. He complained —— me —— the noise of the engine. He brought a complaint —— A. —— the noise of the engine.

Concerned *at* or *about*, *for*, *in*. I am much concerned —— your welfare. I am much concerned —— this business. I am much concerned —— these evil tidings.

Concur *with*, *in*. I concur —— you —— that matter.

Confer *with*, *about*, *on* or *upon*. He conferred a great benefit —— me (*Trans.*). I will confer —— you again —— that matter (*Intrans.*).

Confide *in*, *to*, *of*. I cannot confide this secret —— you (*Trans.*). I confide fully —— your sense of duty (*Intrans.*). I am confident —— success.

Consist *of*, *in*. This book consists (is composed) —— 300 pages. Truthfulness consists (is contained, lies) —— honesty of word, deed, and gesture.

Contemporary *of*, *with*. Burke's career was contemporary —— Sheridan's (*adject.*). Burke was a contemporary —— Sheridan (*used as noun*).

Contrast *to*, *with*. Burke was a great contrast —— Sheridan (*noun*). Burke was contrasted —— Sheridan (*verb*).

Contribution *to*, *towards*. This is my contribution —— that fund. This is my contribution —— that project.

Count *on*, *for*. This counts —— nothing. May I count —— your support.

Deal *by*, *in*, *with*. He dealt well —— his servants. I cannot deal —— such a man any longer. He deals —— salt.

Decision *of*, *on*. He has given his decision —— that case. This is my decision —— the dispute.

Die *of*, *from*, *by*. He died —— overwork. He died —— fever. He died —— violence.

Differ *from, with.* I differ —— you on that subject (person). England differs —— India in climate (thing).

Disappointed *of, in, with.* We are disappointed —— a thing not obtained, —— a thing obtained, —— a person from whom we expected something better.

Discouragement *to, of.* Your discouragement —— him did much harm. Your remarks are a discouragement —— all further effort.

Disqualified *for, from.* He was disqualified by age —— competing. He is disqualified —— that post.

Drop *off, out of.* The soldier dropped —— the line of march. The apple dropped —— the tree.

Eager *for, in.* He was as eager —— the pursuit of knowledge as he was —— distinction.

Embark *on, in.* He has embarked —— a new kind of business. He has embarked —— board ship.

Enamoured *of, with.* He is quite enamoured —— that picture (thing). He is enamoured —— her (person).

End *in, with, by.* He ended his speech —— a fine summing up. The project ended —— failure. He ended the discussion —— declaring that the meeting was dissolved.

Engaged *in, with, to, on.* He has been busily engaged —— me the whole morning. He is engaged —— her. He is deeply engaged —— thought. —— what business were you engaged?

Enter *upon, into.* I cannot enter —— that contract. He has entered —— a new career.

Entrust *with, to.* I shall entrust my money —— him. I shall entrust him —— my money.

Exception *of, to.* There is no exception —— this principle. I make an exception —— this.

Exchange *for, with.* I shall exchange places —— him. I would not exchange my house —— yours.

Excuse *from, for.* I hope I shall be excused —— my absence (pardoned). I hope I shall be excused —— attending (let off).

Experience *in, of.* He has had no experience —— a

storm at sea. I have had much experience —— teaching.

Exult *in, over.* He exults —— me (person). He exults —— my difficulties (thing).

Fail *in, of.* He failed —— that attempt. He failed —— his purpose.

Fall *among, on, into, under, in with.* He fell —— the enemy (attacked them). He fell —— a trance. He fell —— thieves. He fell —— their displeasure. He could fall —— their views (agree to adopt).

False *of, to, in.* He is utterly false —— heart, since he has proved himself false —— his friends (person) and false —— his promises (thing).

Familiar *with, to.* He is familiar —— the subject (thing). The subject is familiar —— him (person).

Favourable *to, for.* The time is favourable —— action. The outlook is not favourable —— his prospects.

Feed *on, with.* The cow feeds —— grass (*Intrans.*). He feeds the cow —— turnips (*Trans.*).

Fight *for, against, with.* There was a long fight —— the flag —— the Confederates.

Note.—"To fight *with*" is ambiguous. We fought *with* (=against) the French at Waterloo. We fought *with* (=on the same side as) the French in the Crimea.

Free *from, of, with.* He is rather too free —— his pen. He is free —— vice of any kind. He is free —— thought.

Furnish *to, with.* He furnished the hungry —— food. He furnished food —— the hungry.

Genius *for, in.* He is a genius —— mathematics. He has a genius —— mathematics.

Get *at, over, out of, to, into, on with.* I cannot get —— him (live or work smoothly with him). He could not get —— the end of his journey in time (finish his journey). He got —— debt, and could not get —— it again. He could not get —— his difficulties (overcome them). We could not get —— the facts (find out the facts).

Glad *of*, *at*. I shall be glad —— his assistance. I was very glad —— the result.

Glance *at*, *over*. He glanced —— the surface. He glanced —— that object.

Grateful *to*, *for*. I was grateful —— him —— that kindness.

Grieve *at* or *about*, *for*. I grieve —— you with all my heart. I felt much grief —— that disaster.

Hardened *against*, *to*. He is hardened —— any feeling of pity. He is hardened —— his debtors.

Heir *to*, *of*. He is the heir —— his uncle (person), and has become heir —— a large estate (thing).

Hold *of*, *on*. A creditor has a hold —— his debtor. Take hold —— that chair.

Impatient *of*, *at*, *for*. He is impatient —— the delay. He is impatient —— food. He is impatient —— control.

Impress *on*, *with*. I impressed him —— that idea. I impressed that idea —— him.

Indebted *to*, *in*, *for*. He was indebted —— a large sum of money. He was indebted —— her —— a large sum of money.

Indignant *at*, *with*. I felt very indignant —— him (person). I was indignant —— his conduct (thing).

Indulge *in*, *with*. He indulges —— wine (*Intrans.*). He indulges himself —— wine (*Trans.*).

Indulgent *in*, *to*. He is too indulgent —— wine. He is too indulgent —— his children.

Influence *over* or *with*, *on*. He has no influence —— me (person). This will have no influence —— the result (thing).

Inquire *into*, *about*, *of*. We will inquire —— him —— this matter. We must inquire —— this mystery.

Interest *in*, *with*. I have no interest —— the Directors of that company. I have a large interest —— that company.

Introduce *to*, *into*. I cannot introduce you —— this society. I will introduce you —— him.

Intrude *upon, into.* He should not intrude —— my privacy. He should not intrude —— my private garden.

Invest *in, with.* He was invested —— full powers. He invested his money —— consols.

Join *in, to.* He joined —— the game (*Intrans.*). He joined one piece of wood —— another (*Trans.*).

Jump *at, to.* It is as foolish to jump —— a conclusion, as it is wise to jump —— an opportunity.

Kick *against, at.* It is not wise to kick —— authority (resist). He kicked his heels —— authority (scornfully rejected).

Labour *at, for, in, under.* He is labouring —— an error. He is labouring —— a good cause. He is labouring —— the public good. He is labouring —— mathematics.

Lavish *of, in.* He was rather too lavish —— his praise. He was lavish —— his expenditure.

Lay *before, to, under.* Lay not this sin —— their charge. He laid me —— an obligation. Lay all the facts —— him.

Lean *against, on, to.* I lean —— this side rather than that. The old man was at one time leaning —— a staff, at another leaning —— a wall.

Level *with, at.* He levelled his gun —— the bird. He levelled the city —— the ground.

Liable *to, for.* All men are liable —— error. He is liable —— payment.

Libel *on, against.* He wrote a libel —— his neighbour. The libel was —— his honesty.

Lie *in, under.* The matter lies —— your own power. I could not consent to lie —— suspicion.

Listen *to, for.* Do not listen —— his complaints. We listened in vain —— the notes of the expected nightingale.

Live *for, by, on, within.* He lives —— honest labour, and well —— his earnings. He lives —— a small income. The highest of virtues is to live —— others.

Look *after*, *at*, *into*, *for*, *over*, *through*, *out of*. He was at that time looking —— the window. This house looks —— the sea (has a wide view of it). Look —— these papers (examine cursorily). Look —— these papers (examine carefully). Look —— every corner (scrutinise closely). Look —— that needle (try to find). Look —— the horse (watch it). A cat may look —— a king.

Make *of*, *for*, *up to*, *away with*. Contentment makes —— happiness (conduces to happiness). He made —— her jewels (stole and carried off). A. made —— B. (approached B. for for some purpose). I can make no meaning —— what he says.

Martyr *to*, *for*. He is a martyr —— rheumatism. He died a martyr —— the cause of liberty.

Moved *at*, *by*, *with*, *to*. She was moved —— tears. They were much moved —— the sight. They were moved —— pity. He was moved —— her entreaties.

Need *for*, *of*. There is no need —— you to repeat this. We are in no need —— assistance.

Negligent *of*, *in*. He is negligent —— his work. He is negligent —— his duties.

Obliged *to*, *for*. I am obliged —— you —— that kindness.

Occupied *with*, *in*. His time was occupied —— many pursuits. He was occupied —— reading a book.

Offence *against*, *at*. That was an offence —— morality. He took offence —— what I said.

Offended *at*, *with*. I am deeply offended —— him (person). I am offended —— his rudeness (thing).

Originate *with*, *from* or *in*. This report originated —— a misunderstanding (thing). It originated —— him (person).

Overcome *with*, *by*. He was overcome —— fatigue. He was overcome —— our entreaties.

Part *from*, *with*. I will not part —— my money (thing), nor do I wish to part —— my friend (person).

Pass *for*, *by*, *over*, *from*, *to* or *into*. Let us pass —— this subject (omit). His mind passes rapidly —— one point —— another. He passes —— a clever man. A carriage passed —— the door.

Play *at*, *on*. He plays well —— cricket. She plays —— the piano.

Point *at*, *to*. This plan points —— almost certain success. Every one points —— him with scorn.

Popular *with*, *for*. He is popular —— his school-fellows —— his good-nature.

Possessed *of*, *with*. His mind is possessed —— that notion. He is possessed —— much wealth.

Preference *for*, *to*. The preference —— wealth —— poverty is almost universal.

Prepared *for*, *against*. We must be prepared —— disaster. Let us be prepared —— action.

Prevail *with* or *upon*, *over* or *against*. He prevailed —— him (persuaded him) to do that. He prevailed —— (defeated) all his enemies.

Preventive *to*, *of*. This drug is preventive —— fever (*adject.*). This drug is a preventive —— fever (*noun*).

Pride *in*, *on*. He prides himself —— his wealth (*verb*). He takes much pride —— his wealth (*noun*).

Proceed *with*, *to*, *against*, *from*. Let us proceed —— the business (the business having been already commenced). Let us proceed —— the business (the business not having been commenced). I shall proceed —— that man (prosecute). This evil result proceeds —— ignorance.

Profuse *of*, *in*. He is as profuse —— his money as he is —— his offers.

Provide *for*, *against*, *with*. We must provide —— the evil day. He must provide —— his children. He was provided —— everything that he wanted.

Quarrel *with*, *between*, *over* or *about*. I have no quarrel —— you. There is no quarrel —— you and me. We need not quarrel —— this little matter.

Quick *of, at.* He is quick —— understanding, and especially quick —— mathematics.

Ready *for, at, in.* He is ready —— his answers, ready —— action, and ready —— accounts.

Reckon *on, with.* I reckon —— your support (confidently expect). I will have a reckoning (settling of accounts) —— you to-morrow.

Reconcile *to, with.* This reconciles me —— you (person). I cannot reconcile the facts —— your statement of them (thing).

Regard *for, to.* I have a great regard —— his character. With regard —— that point we must agree to differ.

Rejoice *in, at.* He is one who rejoices not only —— his own happiness, but —— that of another.

Remonstrate *with, against.* He remonstrated —— him —— his conduct.

Repose *on, in.* He is reposing —— a bed (*Intrans.*). He reposes full confidence —— me (*Trans.*).

Requisite *to, for.* We must do what is requisite —— the purpose. Do what is requisite —— success.

Resolve *on, into.* Air can be resolved —— its elements. He is resolved —— a course of action.

Respect *of, to, for.* I have no respect —— him. With respect —— that matter let us say no more. In respect —— that quality he surpasses you.

Responsible *to, for.* I am not responsible —— you —— what I do or say.

Rest *on, with, from.* It rests —— you to do what seems best. I must rest a little —— this chair. He gets no rest —— suffering.

Result *from, in, of.* This is the result —— laziness (*noun*). This results —— laziness (*verb*). Laziness results —— ruin.

Revenge *on, for.* They revenged themselves —— him —— the injury.

Run *after, at, into, over, through.* The dog ran —— the cat (pursued). The dog ran —— the cat (attacked). He ran —— debt. Let us run ——

the accounts (read rapidly). He ran —— his money (spent all of it).

Rupture *with*, *between*. He had a rupture —— me. There was a rupture —— him and me.

Satisfied *of*, *with*. I am satisfied —— the fact (convinced). I am satisfied —— his work (contented).

Search *for*, *after*, *of*. He is in search —— an occupation. We made a search —— the lost jewel. Most men make a search —— happiness.

Secure *from*, *against*. He is secure —— harm, and —— all attacks.

Set *about*, *over*, *upon*. The dog set —— the cat (attacked). He set —— the business (commenced). He was set —— the business (placed in charge of it).

Slave *of*, *to*. He is a slave —— avarice (*Indef. art.*). He is the slave —— avarice (*Def. art.*).

Smile *at*, *upon*. We can smile —— your threats. Success smiled —— our efforts (favoured).

Solicitous *of* or *about*, *for*. I am solicitous —— the future. I am solicitous —— your welfare.

Speak *of*, *on*. He spoke —— that subject (briefly). He spoke —— that subject (at greater length).

Speculate *in*, *on*. He speculated —— cotton (risked his money). He speculated —— an uncertainty.

Stand *against*, *by*, *on*, *to*. He stood —— his opinion (maintained). He stood —— his dignity. He stood —— his friend (supported). He stood —— the enemy (resisted).

Stare *at*, *in*. He stared —— me. He stared me —— the face.

Stick *at*, *to*. He sticks —— his point. He sticks —— nothing.

Strike *at*, *for*, *on*. The ship struck —— a rock. The men struck —— higher pay. He struck —— the dog.

Suitable *to*, *for*. His speech was suitable —— the occasion. The book is suitable —— the purpose.

Supply *to*, *with*. They supplied water —— the thirsty

(person). They supplied the thirsty —— water (thing).

Take *after*, *for*, *to*, *upon*. He took —— himself to give me a lecture. He took me —— a stranger. He has taken —— gambling. He takes —— his father (is growing like him in pursuits, appearance, etc.).

Talk *of* or *about*, *to* or *with*, *over*. Let me talk —— you for a few minutes. Let us talk —— this matter (discuss fully). Did he talk —— coming back (allude to briefly)?

Taste *of*, *for*. Now we shall have a taste —— hard work (some experience of hard work). He has no taste (liking) —— music.

Think *of*, *over* or *on*. He never thought —— that (momentary thinking). He thought well —— the subject (sustained or prolonged thinking).

Tired *of*, *with*. He is tired —— waiting. He is tired —— his exertions.

Touch *at*, *upon*. The ship touched —— Gibraltar. Let us now now touch —— this subject (briefly allude to).

Trespass *in*, *on*, *against*. Do not trespass —— a man's time or —— his house. He trespassed —— the rule.

Trust *in*, *to*, *with*. I trust —— your honour (*Intrans.*). I trust —— you (*Intrans.*). I trust you —— money (*Trans.*). I trust this money —— your care (*Trans.*).

Use *of*, *for*, *in*. We have no use —— that. There is no use —— that. What is the use —— that?

Victim *of*, *to*. He is a victim —— oppression (*Indef. art.*). He is the victim —— oppression (*Def. art.*).

Wait *at*, *for*, *on*. We must wait —— the next train. We have no one to wait —— us (attend to our wants). He knows how to wait —— table.

Warn *of*, *against*. He was warned —— his danger. He was warned —— A.'s designs.

Wary *in*, *of*. He was wary —— that man's designs (guarded against and prepared to meet). He is wary —— all that he does.

(*b*) *Fill up the gap in each sentence, putting in or leaving out the preposition after the verb, according to the requirements of idiom :—*

Admit, admit of. Such conduct —— no excuse. I cannot —— the excuse that you have offered.

Attend, attend to. He will —— the meeting. He will —— the business of the meeting.

Bear, bear with. We must —— his reproaches (endure patiently). We must —— his reproaches (endure).

Begin, begin with. Let us —— this song (commence to sing it). Let us —— this song (sing this song before singing any other).

Believe, believe in. I do not —— this man (trust in his honesty). I do not —— this man (accept his statement as true).

Call, call on. I have —— him (visited him at his house). I have —— him (ordered him to come).

Catch, catch at. He —— the reins (seized). He —— the reins (tried to seize).

Close, close with. I cannot —— such a bargain (accept). This —— the bargain (concludes).

Commence, commence with. We must —— this work (begin to do it). We must —— this work (do this before doing any other).

Consult, consult with. I must —— you on this point (ask your advice). I must —— you on this point (take counsel with you).

Count, count on. Have you —— the money (reckoned up). I —— that money (expect it as a certainty).

Deal, deal in. He —— cards (sells). He —— the cards (distributes them to the different players).

Dispense, dispense with. We can —— your charities (do not require). He —— his charities fairly (distributes).

Eat, eat into. Mice —— cheese (make a hole in it by eating). Mice —— cheese (use it as food).

Feel, feel for. The blind man —— the table (tries to find the table by groping for it with his hand). We —— the hardness of the table (are made conscious of it by the sense of touch).

Gain, gain on. He —— the land (reached). The sea —— the land (washes it down, encroaches on it).

Grasp, grasp at. He —— the money (attempted to seize it). He —— the money (held it firmly in his hand).

Guard, guard against. We must —— him from danger (protect). We must —— danger (take precautions).

Guess, guess at. He —— the facts (tried to find them out by guessing). He —— the facts (found out by guessing).

Inquire, inquire into. He —— the reason (investigated it). He —— the reason (asked what it was).

Meditate, meditate on. He —— revenge (future action). He —— the revenge that he took (past action).

Meet, meet with. I —— him on the way (found him accidentally). I —— him on the way (came in front of him).

Prepare, prepare for. He —— a feast (got it ready). He —— the feast (got himself ready).

Repair, repair to. Let us —— the house (go). Let us —— the house (do it up).

Search, search for. You must —— the thief (find out where he is). You must —— the thief (examine everything that is on him).

Send, send for. They have —— the doctor (summoned). They have —— the doctor (despatched).

Touch, touch upon. He —— the point (briefly alluded to it). He has scarcely —— the point (come to it).

Work, work at. He —— the machine (managed it). He —— the machine (was engaged with it).

SECTION 6.—TO SUBSTITUTE ONE PART OF SPEECH FOR ANOTHER.

84. Interchange of Nouns, Verbs, Adjectives, and Adverbs.—A sentence can be recast in such a way that the same radical word can be used in one version as a noun, in another as a verb, in another as an adjective, in another as an adverb:—

He was much *annoyed* at hearing such remarks.
The hearing of such remarks gave him much *annoyance.*

Lead and tin *differ* very greatly in weight.
Between lead and tin there is much *difference* in weight.
The weight of lead is very *different* from that of tin.

He was very *free* with his money.
He parted very *freely* with his money.

Exercises on § 84. (To be done orally and at sight.)

(*a*) *Recast* (*without altering the sense*) *the following sentences, substituting the* **Verb**-*form for each of the words italicised. The verb may be either Finite or non-Finite* :—

1. Two friends took a *journey* together through a forest.
2. On the way the *approach* of a grisly bear was seen.
3. One of them had no *thought* for his friend's safety.
4. He climbed up a tree with all possible *haste*,
5. and sought *concealment* among the branches.
6. The other man threw himself down on *pretence* of being dead;
7. for bears have no *liking* for the flesh of a corpse.
8. The bear took a *sniff* at every part of him;
9. but finding that there was no *movement* in any of his limbs,
10. it went away without doing him any *harm*.

11. Then the man hidden in the tree made his *descent*.

12. "It came to my *notice*," said he, "while I was in the tree,

13. that the bear's nose was almost in *touch* with your ear. Did the bear tell you anything?"

14. "Yes," said the other, "the bear told me a *valuable* secret.

15. He told me to avoid in future the company of those

16. who in time of danger think only of their own *safety*."

17. *Apparently* we shall not see you here again.

18. His speech was received with universal *applause*.

19. His conduct met with general *approval* and *praise*.

20. We had better not have an *argument* about this.

21. I cannot give my *assent* to this proposal.

22. His conversation gave us much *amusement*.

23. He had an *allowance* of £60 a year from his father.

24. He made a long *search* for the watch, but in vain.

25. He gave three *repetitions* of the blow.

26. We must take some *rest* before we go any further.

27. This hedge is the western *boundary* of my farm.

28. There is a *jingle* of money in that room.

29. He has a *hatred* for vice of every kind.

30. We must show *obedience* to our betters.

31. He took a *step* forward in the dark.

32. I have no *love* for underhand methods.

33. He had a long and sound *sleep* last night.

34. I have no *fear* of the consequences.

35. His objections were received by us with *laughter*.

36. The *tillage* of the soil is the work of husbandmen.

37. The Chinese built the Great Wall for *defence*.

38. I had the *choice* of four different books.

39. Sun-*rise* is at six o'clock.

40. The horse took a *run* across the meadow.

41. I view your conduct with deep *regret*.

42. It gives me much *pleasure* to hear you sing.

43. He made a long *stay* in this house.

44. The *seizure* of his goods was a painful *sight* to him.

45. I have no *expectation* or *intention* of staying here.

46. He gave me no *admission* into his room.
47. All my arguments failed to produce *conviction*.
48. I am willing to express *forgiveness*.
49. Make a *beginning*, and do not leave off in a *hurry*.
50. I can do this with your *assistance*.
51. You will have to pay a *fine* for an *infraction* of the law.
52. The *infliction* of a fine on you gives me *pain*.
53. Dismiss your *fears*: all will be well in the *end*.
54. Fix your *attention* on the work in hand.
55. The story was given in *speech*, not in *writing*.
56. He had no *control* over his temper.
57. He gave an *order* that the door should be closed at eight.
58. I will give you all the *support* and *protection* that I can.
59. The *advice* that he gave them was sound.
60. It is not my *belief* that this man will be *prosperous*.
61. *Condolence* does not always produce *consolation*.
62. I will not give you any more *trouble*.
63. Come, let us see the *abode* of the hermit.
64. These flowers are now in blossom.
65. One steamer came into *collision* with the other.

(*b*) *Recast* (*without altering the sense*) *the following sentences, substituting the* **Noun**-*form for each of the words italicised* :—

1. The one refused to be *corrected* by the other.
2. After cutting down that tree I feel much *fatigued*.
3. The term for which I was *engaged* has nearly expired.
4. He insisted that his view was quite *accurate*.
5. He *argued* and *discussed* for a long time before he yielded.
6. He *based* his hopes on a plentiful supply of recruits.
7. He was *exhausted* with his long ride.
8. I do not *expect* or even *intend* to stay long in this house.
9. They were much *surprised* and *vexed* at the news.
10. The monkeys were *headed* by an old grey chieftain.

11. They were *officered* like so many soldiers.
12. This rock *projects* a long way out towards the sea.
13. We will *commence* work at this point.
14. The sound gradually *increased*, as we advanced.
15. Do not be too *reliant* on other men's help.
16. He carried on his studies very *successfully*.
17. Tell me *candidly* what your object is.
18. Several persons *aided* the cause of temperance.
19. The rain *continued* the whole of that day.
20. The bridge is now practically *completed*.
21. The troop *passed* over the bridge in safety.
22. This problem cannot be *solved*.
23. This play has *delighted* us all.
24. What does he *mean* by such rudeness?
25. He threw down his tools and *defied* the foreman.
26. He is not *empowered* to give such an order.
27. Have you ever *tried* this new method.
28. *Govern* your tongue; this is very necessary.
29. He can *behave* very well, if he chooses.
30. Such conduct *disgraced* the whole family.
31. He is *sensible* enough to keep aloof from bad company.
32. I am not *acquainted* with him even distantly.
33. The owner is ready to *sell* this horse and carriage.
34. He has been *inimical* to me for a long time past.
35. There is nothing *stable* in his character.
36. I believe in his being entirely *innocent*.
37. This water must be *filtrated* before it is drunk.
38. To eat and drink *temperately* is one secret of health.
39. He was not *polite* enough to stand aside.
40. He is very *influential* in Parliament.
41. He went as a *pilgrim* to the Holy Land.
42. She is not very *graceful* in her movements.
43. He *troubled* me very much with his complaints.
44. There was no reason for him to *complain*.
45. They *frolicked* in the garden for more than an hour.
46. He *contracted* with the builder for the erection of the house.
47. The house was half hidden in a *shady* valley.

48. Can you *prove* what you say?

49. It is pleasanter to *approve* than to *reprove*: so all men should strive to *improve* themselves.

50. This black cloud makes the room *gloomy*.

51. A poor man must be *frugal* in his habits.

52. I cannot endure such *tyrannical* treatment.

53. Would you like to *peruse* this letter?

54. He did not *scruple* to desert me.

55. To *betray* a friend is disgraceful.

56. That *stupid* student *tries* my patience.

57. Gentleness will not tame a *furious* tiger.

58. He was *treacherous* enough to desert his friends.

59. He has *flattered* rather than *praised* me.

60. The streams of that county *abound* in fish.

61. He will conquer if he *perseveres*.

62. His professions are *sincere*, I do not *doubt*.

63. Where England is *supreme* is on the sea.

64. He *judged* of the case very severely.

65. These goods *sold* well at the auction.

66. He is not one of those in whom I *confide*.

67. As the judge *suggested*, the complaint was dismissed.

68. I am not *satisfied* with his excuses.

69. The witness stated that he *abhorred* such conduct.

70. The committee urged that A. should be *dismissed*.

71. To *accomplish* this task we must make every effort.

72. Such a thing does not *occur* every day.

73. You must not depend upon me to *maintain* you.

74. The one brother does not at all *resemble* the other.

(*c*) *Recast* (*without altering the sense*) *the following sentences, substituting the* **Adjective**-*form for each of the words italicised*:—

1. This rain will give fresh *fertility* to the soil.
2. He *presumes* to think that he stands first.
3. *Plenty* of rain fell yesterday.
4. In a great *crisis* like this we cannot be too careful.
5. The barking of that dog gives us much *trouble*.
6. He is rather inclined to *quarrel*.
7. This gentleman represents the *opposition*.

8. We waited with much *curiosity* to see the result.
9. There is *likelihood* of rain falling to-day.
10. This river is not more than four feet in *depth*.
11. Animals with four *legs* are the most useful.
12. He is *unusually* eloquent as a speaker.
13. He has too much *impulse* and not enough *caution*.
14. Mildew will do much *mischief* to the fruit.
15. A minstrel of great *age* came to the door.
16. Quicken your pace, and move a little more *nimbly*.
17. My sister has much *simplicity* of character.
18. Have *patience* and *hope* in time of *sickness*.
19. The thickness of the timber gives it *strength*.
20. Why was there so much *coldness* in his manner.
21. He has not *humility* enough to apologise.
22. The *heat* of this air will dry up the plants.
23. He takes much *pride* in the position that he holds.
24. Make the best use of your time in *youth*.
25. This wall is two feet in *width* and six in *height*.
26. *Poverty* is often treated with contempt.
27. The walk was of such *length* that it tired me.
28. He is a man of strict *justice* and *impartiality*.
29. The river is nearly a quarter of a mile in *breadth*.
30. A man is rewarded for deeds of *truth* and *honesty*.
31. His policy was marked by *wisdom* and *prudence*.
32. No sound was heard in the *stillness* of the night.
33. He had *generosity* enough to spare the guilty.
34. He acted with the courage of a *hero*.
35. I want some plaster that will *adhere*.
36. We cannot but *despise* his motives.
37. He has not yet *completed* his explanation.
38. His conduct does not deserve *censure*.
39. His conduct appears to be beyond *reproach*.
40. He was not *compelled* to come here to-day.
41. He has no *decision* of character.
42. Which of these two is most worthy of *blame?*
43. His reputation is in *peril:* help him, if you can.
44. His *apprehensions* were keener than they need have been.
45. The thought could not be *effaced* from his memory.

46. In liberality he is without a *rival*.
47. The inner garment was made of *wool*.
48. His last years were spent in *peace* and *tranquillity*.
49. There is no *necessity* for such excitement.
50. He was remarkable for his *humanity*.
51. There will be no *passage* through the road for the next week.
52. He has had much *practice* in debate.
53. The *density* of the forest retarded our progress.
54. He shows no *penitence* for his fault.
55. Was there anything worth *noticing* in his manner?
56. He often *changes* his mind.
57. His temper is one that cannot be *managed*.
58. He *volunteered* his help; no one asked for it.
59. Some birds *migrate* with the change of season.
60. With all his *cleverness* he failed in the examination.
61. He lived in *solitude* in that lonely tower.
62. He devoted himself to *literature*.
63. The *splendour* of his retinue surprised them.
64. The workmen *clamoured* for better pay.
65. London is a city with a large *population*.
66. Napoleon's return from Moscow was full of *disaster*.
67. Athens was wholly given to *idolatry*.
68. His speech was worthy of *contempt* and nothing else.
69. He was a man of great *courage* and *energy*.

(*d*) *Recast (without altering the sense) the following sentences, substituting the* **Adverb**-*form for each of the words italicised*:—

1. Eric was allowed to roam in *freedom* through the forest.
2. He was advised to invest his money with much *caution*.
3. In an *instant* the signal was given, and all set off.
4. His action was *adverse* to our interests.
5. There was a *gradual* increase in the number.
6. He struck his hand with *violence* on the table.
7. He *surprised* us with his rude manners.
8. He showed much *patience* in his sufferings.

9. He had a very *narrow* escape of being caught.
10. He wrote to me a *confidential* letter on the subject.
11. To live with *temperance* is the secret of living long.
12. The *early* bird finds the worm.
13. He has lived a *virtuous* life throughout.
14. It was a *fortunate* thing that no one was hurt.
15. He spent his days in *idleness* at home.
16. Boys should *respect* their teachers.
17. She gave him a *cold* reception, and he *deserved* it.
18. Your action was *unkind* as well as *unwise.*
19. The *precise* meaning of his words is unknown to us.
20. The cripple sat every *day* at the gate.
21. There seems to be much *discord* in that house.
22. He drew out the tooth with a great deal of *skill.*
23. He spoke with much *bitterness* of the injustice done to him.
24. He *stole* out of the house, when no one was awake.
25. I wrote him an *official* letter on the subject.
26. He set to work with much *energy* and much *caution.*
27. His work is as *efficient* as it is *useful.*
28. You must work with more *expedition.*
29. His behaviour *vexes* me sometimes.
30. He spoke with more *malice* than *kindness.*
31. He acted with more *ambition* than *judgment.*
32. Bees spread their wax with much *sagacity.*
33. Twenty applicants came forward in *succession.*
34. It is a source of *happiness* to us that he recovered.
35. The growth of a seed is too gradual to be *perceived.*
36. The time we spent there gave us much *pleasure.*
37. His action was quite *independent* of my advice.

THE END